A CRY FOR HELP

STEPHEN DRAKE

First Century Ltd, 27 Greenhead Road, Huddersfield, West Yorkshire HD1 4EN.

Website: www.first-century.co.uk

E mail: Info@first-century.co.uk

ISBN 1-903930-36-7

Chapter 1

The train drew up at the dimly-lit station, disturbing the tranquillity of the night in the small village. Charlie Lloyd pressed the green button and the automatic doors opened. He jumped to the platform grasping his large plastic bag that contained a few personal belongings. He ambled to the exit and as no guard was on duty he tossed his partly chewed ticket onto the concrete. Was he heading for a new beginning? He felt anxious, perhaps even nauseous. Part of him needed to cry as a newborn baby torn from the security of his mother's womb. A young child lost in a strange city craving a familiar face. The nervous anticipation gradually developed over many days now threatened to take him prisoner. He struggled to relax, to think positively.

"Nothing will ruin my life," he encouraged himself. "I ain't gonna be controlled by anything."

His mood altered as his spirits heightened. Maybe, just maybe, he could belong in the free world, a few trusty friends, an enjoyable job, a career even.

"Yes," he mused, "I'm gonna take this chance by the bollocks and hang on."

He moved swiftly through the crowd, many people hurrying to reach home after a hustling day. It was already dusky and no one liked walking about after dark.

"Lots of funny people about," Charlie smiled to himself. "Bloody good job they can't read my mind."

He passed a smartly dressed gentleman who carried an umbrella and a briefcase. The individual glanced momentarily at Charlie and continued about his business. Charlie looked away almost immediately; he certainly didn't want anyone to think that he was staring at them. He had come to realise that with his aggressive appearance, it paid to be cautious.

"'Never judge a book by its cover.' Haven't any of these city types heard of that?"

Charlie strolled between two young women, obviously friends, hauling several bulky shopping bags. Of immaculate appearance the pair had probably spent their husbands' hard earned sterling in the city.

"Ain't it strange how pretty birds always pull blokes with lots of dosh," Charlie thought, as he studied the attractive couple. "If matey was on the jam role they probably wouldn't give him the time of day."

Somebody nudged into Charlie as he trudged homewards. He sharply glanced around to catch sight of a stooped, grey-haired old lady. This sweet, harmless pensioner could have been the Devil as for the effect she had on Charlie.

"Oh God," the thought burst into his brain, "did I punch her?"

Inside his head he unwillingly pictured the scenario. Tears from his mother as she tried to come to terms with the monster she had raised. Disgust from his sister who always looked upon her brother as a respectable criminal. Disbelief from his mates who saw him as a nice bloke, maybe a little wayward. And his own disgust, how could he live with hurting such a defenceless human. He attentively watched the elderly lady, completely unharmed, shuffle on her way.

"What if she collapses later," he panicked as utter dread built-up inside him.

He visibly trembled: beads of perspiration were noticeable on his face and his heart felt like a sledgehammer pounding against his chest. He remained static while trying to calm himself. He knew that he mustn't lose control; he had to stay as relaxed as he could command. Several minutes elapsed before his heartbeat slowed, feeling returned to his extremities and he could rationalise about his situation. A wave of depression swept over the young man. His spirit was battered but not quite broken. He knew, from experience, that he was at the top of a slippery slope. He must fight for his sanity. Depression made him vulnerable. Vulnerability opened the door to unwanted ideas. These thoughts increased his depression. He must get a grip. Break the circle before it began. He rubbed his blue eyes with a damp hand. He knew he wouldn't weep; these frightening intrusions were yet to gain such satisfaction - they never would. Nobody likes to feel depressed and Charlie was no exception. He understood that he would worry about his 'victim' for many hours if not days. The black cloud still hung heavily but gradually a red mist took its place.

"Why me? Why now?" he cursed, "people see me as a bit of a laugh, someone with a bit of bottle, but, fuck it, they don't know shit. They can't see a fucked-up idiot who hasn't got a life."

He marched towards his habitation, the plastic bag slung over his shoulder.

"Fuck. Fuck. Fuck." he swore, "I just want to be normal." He pounded the pavement. "So what if I had smacked the old bag" he spat the words knowing that his anger was totally misdirected.

He didn't care. Maybe that wasn't true. As the words of fury passed his lips his left hand grasped his right. He knew the reason - he certainly wasn't going to strike an old woman. No chance. The road was quiet with fields on one side and trees the other.

"Did you hit that woman?" Charlie asked himself yet again. "Can you remember punching her?"

He replayed the moment in his mind attempting to ease his fears.

"No, I can't picture myself clumping her," he answered his own question.

"What if you did harm her in some way," the voice, presumably his, forced an entrance.

Charlie, too concerned with his own predicament, ignored the distant sounds of laughter. He failed to notice the three youths until he walked into them. Maybe he had seen them but, being so on edge, didn't care. He wouldn't even deny walking into the group on purpose. What had he got to lose?

"Watch it, mate," shouted one of the group, "why can't you look where you're going?"

"Get fucked," Charlie growled, in no mood for sensible suggestions.

He wasn't scared of their reaction, his mind being filled with more urgent matters. It wouldn't have bothered the young man if he finished the evening in a casualty department; all he craved was reassurance that he hadn't assaulted the elderly female. While that concern occupied his thoughts, nothing else was of importance. This single-minded approach exasperated the stocky youth - it took a great deal to infuriate Charlie but where much had failed, his deranged thought process succeeded. He attempted to push pass the gang who prevented his progress. Caution had been thrown to the wind - why

5

should he show respect to others when his own mind was intent on destruction.

"Move," he ordered.

He wasn't stupid. He knew that his behaviour was provocative and totally unfair. What did he care? Life wasn't very fair to him, was it? They stood their ground, obviously feeling they had been harshly treated. How were they to know that this young man was behaving completely out of character? He looked like trouble, didn't he? Probably the type of bloke who thrived on violence. Charlie stepped forward again. This time one of the bunch, a tall lad of average build, grabbed his shoulder. Charlie didn't hesitate. Quickly swinging with his opposite hand he smashed the youth accurately on the nose, forcing the man to release his grip. Charlie recognised the pattern. His anxiety drove him into action. Not usually the instigator of unprovoked fighting, without his lingering worry this confrontation would never have taken place. If it had then Charlie would have been the victim, not the aggressor.

"Don't touch me." snarled Charlie, confident that he had scared the pathetic mob witless

How wrong can you be? Charlie felt a firm punch to the back of the head. He staggered forward, dropping his hands to the pavement to prevent him from falling. He turned to face the gang member who had delivered the blow, just in time to receive a second strike that split open both his lips.

"Bugger me," he thought, "I'm getting what was due. Don't start something you can't finish. Bit late for bloody advice."

Blood poured from his mouth and he could taste the warm liquid trickling down his throat. He felt dizzy, his head pounded and he desperately tried to remain upright. Isn't it strange what some people think about in times of crisis?

"One good thing," rebounded around Charlie's skull, "at least I'm worrying about reality and not fantasy. I haven't given that old biddy a thought since me and this lot started getting to know each other."

He failed to see which youth smashed his cheek sending him crashing to the pavement.

"Stay down, stay down." he told himself.

He lay on *terra firma* and covered his shaven head with his hands to limit the damage that would be caused by the inevitable blows to follow.

The three assailants savagely struck out at the groaning figure.

"Fucking wanker, stupid bastard, flaming shit," they yelled, "don't ever mess with us."

These chaps obviously hadn't mastered the control and restraint technique. They certainly didn't consider personal problems as they handed their victim a thrashing.

Charlie opened his eyes and gazed at the dark, clear, night sky.

"A well deserved beating," he mused. "As far as they were concerned I was bang out of order. If they hadn't given me a slap they'd have looked stupid. I ain't got no complaints. Even if they had known I was some nutter who worried about punching old women they would have still knocked me about for being a weirdo."

Charlie judged himself harshly. The thoughts that he couldn't control classified him as a lunatic. In his opinion he deserved everything he received. He made no excuses. A caring person might have suggested mental illness but not Charlie. He viewed his problem as, simply, a wicked side to his nature. He didn't have cancer, heart disease or any other physical ailment. No, he was just a bad, bad person, a nutcase who deserved to suffer for the evil ideas that developed inside his head. The slight matter that, as far as he knew, he had never acted upon these thoughts didn't arise. Wasn't it bad enough to have such wickedness within one's person? Still, he was alive unless, of course, he had passed to a different sphere.

"When I die," he wondered, "if there is something after this bloody life then, maybe, I will be normal. What a lovely thought. Not shitting myself whenever I see some old dear."

He pinched his throbbing leg, which burned to the touch confirming his suspicions that he had survived the beating. The young man was, obviously, pleased to be in the land of the living. Still, it has to be said that a part of him was saddened the struggle with himself would continue. A person at war with himself.

"If this walk home was to have been his final exit he could at least rest in peace," he mused.

He likened his complaint to a person who is constantly in the company of their worst enemy. Never being given the chance to relax, always on guard, waiting for the inevitable attack. He knelt on all fours, regaining his breath, before the major test of standing-up. He noticed his bag, untouched, a few yards from the incident.

"Well, at least they ain't thieves," muttered Charlie, "just a few likely lads out for a good night who ain't prepared to let some loon take the piss."

He forced himself upright causing immense discomfort to his battered torso, but he knew it was an evil necessity.

"Did he deserve all this pain and aggro," he murmured, feeling an overwhelming sense of distress, sadness even.

He felt empty. Surrounded by darkness inside as well as outside. He managed a few steps, nothing broken, so reaching his intended destination would be within his capabilities. He gathered his luggage and struggled onwards. Surely, little else could go wrong. Since leaving the train station he had acquired a worry that wouldn't because concern for your average individual but caused great stress for Charlie, acted upon the vexation and, to complete a memorable journey, ended-up flattened on the pavement. The house was a welcoming sight. A refuge from the outside world. A place where he could find peace - hopefully free from old women, and all thoughts of the older generation. He unlocked his front door and stumbled into the property.

"I don't reckon I'd have made it much further," Charlie reflected, "especially after the day I've had. Ain't it amazing how something can go so wrong, so bloody quickly? I suppose that you can't expect much else when you're fighting a continual battle inside your head."

He chucked his belongings all over the carpeted floor and collapsed onto the leather sofa. He rested his bleeding head in his hands and could only watch as the red liquid dripped onto the dark blue carpet.

"Reasons to be cheerful?" Charlie asked himself, rubbing his scarred hand across his broken nose.

"Well, when that geezer broke my conk, times were bad. They got better then and they will now," he tried to encourage himself.

He desperately tried to think positively. Yet he, who always offered a smile and a kind word, was finding it increasingly difficult not to rip the room to pieces.

"What the fuck's happened to me?" he thought. "I wish someone would tell me what I have done to deserve this."

Chapter 2

"7A's, 2 B's and a C" Mr. Stevenson, the well respected and equally liked maths master, informed the expectant twelve year old pupil, who was fidgeting nervously.

A grin spread over Charlie Lloyd's face, the air automatically expelled from his lungs came out as a huge sigh of relief. These results were expected to be good, but success on this scale was really quite exceptional.

"Wonderful" reflected Charlie, "I've made it.

Everyone, my parents, friends and teachers, told me that I had the ability to do well - now I've proved it to them and myself. Even if I was slightly lacking in self belief, all that extra studying and continual effort has certainly been worthwhile."

Charlie spoke to his closest friend of the last four years, Toby, who had also done well.

"Thank the Lord for that," he commented.

"Yes," agreed Toby, "I'd be a liar if I said we were anything other than brilliant."

"Did you get an 'A' grade in French?" Charlie asked.

"Oui," said his friend. "I think that most of the class got their best mark 'en francais'. All that suffering at the hands of Mr. Baker was, obviously, a necessary evil."

"No more Monsieur Baker," Charlie thought. "At least I won't sit in his lessons scared that I've forgotten to do a piece of homework. I will no longer have to tell my friends that I love foreign languages and enjoyed perfecting my homework when really I was just petrified of the teacher."

Every pupil had a healthy respect for Mr. Baker, if you were a bright, conscientious schoolboy or an idle loafer with a great dislike of homework, or any work for that matter, you would still take the time to make sure you studied the necessary French text. Committing to memory the past tense of 'aller' had to be much more important than taking a spotty teenage girl to the cinema.

Charlie was thrilled with his 'A' grade in science. What he had lacked in ability he had compensated with hard graft.

"I reckon I deserved top marks," he thought to himself, "I drove myself, with some much needed help from Mrs. Hall, and even when people reasoned I'd done enough I still carried-on. I was called a swot, teacher's pet and more besides but I'm the one who feels good now. Anyway, I wasn't going to let Toby get better marks than me - was I?"

Charlie was pleased that his friend had done well just as long as he had done better. Charlie's worst result was in geography. He had kept his nose in front of his rivals and that was enough. Geography lessons were not seen as a time to discuss the British Isles but as periods of riotous fun and frolics. The teacher, a pleasant lady in her forties, had no control over her class. After a stressful French period, geography was just what the doctor ordered. A time to tell jokes, let off steam (and wind) and generally create controlled mayhem. Poor Mrs. Taylor, quite often, left the classroom fighting-away the tears. Pupils - more like bloody football hooligans.

"I really hope that Mrs. Taylor is okay," mused Charlie, "just because she was soft was no reason for us to take advantage. Now, I wish I had behaved and not fooled around to be the same as the others."

He admitted that a 'C' grade was far more than he deserved - in fact, if he had been unable to find the toilets it would have been his own fault.

Charlie and Toby thought back to another part of their school life - sporting achievements. They were both first team players in the three major sports - cricket, rugby and football. They had each striven to better the other thus reaching a high standard.

"They say that fierce competition makes you improve," reflected Charlie, "and I think that my single minded determination to topple Toby has made me a better student and sportsman."

Toby and Charlie were both to go to fee-paying schools although, for reasons beyond their control, they were not to be continuing their education together.

"I hope that I make some equally good friends," thought Charlie. "A person who will push me to the limits. I like Toby very much, so I suppose that's what makes it so important to be better than him."

Was this healthy competition or an unhealthy fixation?

11

Charlie was once again spoken to by Old Stevo. "Your results are the best for ten years at this school. Well done. All your masters have predicted a great future."

Charlie knew that he had earned this moment. He had been neurotic about his lessons. A history essay would be flawless - nothing less was passable; perfection was essential. A French comprehension could not contain one mistake - nothing but full marks were, in his mind, acceptable. Nothing could ruin this day - life was wonderful. Was it really possible for a virgin to feel so much pleasure? Charlie's obsessive desire to be academically competent had been reached. He had forsaken all pleasures to achieve such success. Boys of greater ability had gained lesser marks. Charlie glowed from the top of the tree but could he remain in the highest branch when other distractions tried to make him fall? And, if he were to tumble, then surely it was unlikely that he would land on another high branch. Now, all he wanted to think about was a good school and wasn't everyone saying that if he continued in the same manner then he should excel.

The holidays began slowly, as a middle distance runner, and then sprinted towards the end. All too soon, the shops were stocking everything required for a return to school. The new school term at Epsom saw the arrival of a scruffy pupil with untidy blonde hair. He was fairly popular among his peers and had many friends of varied academic abilities. He studied quite hard to maintain a respectable position in the top groups but, if he were completely honest with himself, could not compete with the most able students. Charlie was aware that increased effort was warranted but found himself drawn to the idea of some particular friends rather than academic excellence. These friends were not necessarily a good influence rather a good ego boost. Lots of good-looking girls and illegal drinking.

"I know that I should put more effort into studying than trying to impress some of the guys," thought Charlie, but it didn't take long to shove his conscience to one side and start to worry about the latest haircut. Who cares about photosynthesis?

Was this the beginning of the end of Charlie's neurotic desire to be a budding scholar?

One Tuesday afternoon, as the sun began to break through the clouds, Charlie observed a scribbled notice informing all new pupils that, if interested, they would be able to try their hand at the very physically demanding game of squash.

"Should be a laugh," Charlie enthused to his friend, Bill, "I'll have a quick knock about before I get my head stuck in a book for the evening."

William nodded his agreement. He was of lesser academic ability but a pleasant fun-loving pupil. He was small with appealing features and an athletic build. The type of chap that made girls feel maternal. The two boys arrived at the courts later that afternoon. Charlie was fascinated by the speed and quickness of thought that the game demanded.

"Amazing," mused Charlie, as he watched two older boys struggle to win an impressive point.

Charlie and William started to knock-up. Mistakes were made frequently but with the passing of time all aspects of the game improved.

"This game is something else," thought Charlie as he struck the small, green ball, "to be good at a sport like this would be really brilliant."

After about twenty-five minutes both youths were covered in perspiration. They had both enjoyed this introduction to a new pastime. Charlie, however, might already have decided this game would be more than a pastime. He shook William's dripping palm, pulled open the old wooden door and stepped off the court.

"What a superb game," he thought to himself, "I really would love to reach the standard of some of the older boys. Better still, I would love to beat them all. When I put my mind to something I usually get there so I shall work at my game whenever I get a chance. I'm going to try and become an exceptional player and, then, who knows?"

As these ideas whirled around the pupil's head he felt, somehow, strange. It was a weird sensation. Yes, he might fail in his attempts to be British champion but he would certainly achieve the highest standard his ability allowed. Almost immediately nothing else was of paramount importance- an obsession had been born. Charlie spent more time than would be considered healthy, thinking about squash.

He constantly thought how he could further his ability. He read magazines and books about the sport becoming quite an expert about the game's top players. Whenever he found time to browse round the shops he studied rackets and shoes. He saved all his spare cash and after careful consideration purchased the racket that, he felt, would be best for him. Jahangir Khan - your days on top are numbered.

"Of course I didn't mean that you were too thin," said Charlie, "you've got a lovely body."

"Do you really mean that?" asked Sonia.

"Sure I do," replied Charlie, his mind replaying a drop-shot winner.

"But earlier you said I was too skinny and all my bumps were in the wrong places," Sonia persisted.

"I guess I was in a bad mood," soothed Charlie. "Had an awful day."

"You mean you played a bad game of squash," answered Sonia, very familiar with the ways of her boyfriend.

"You're right, I'm really sorry," said Charlie, "but you're a lovely girl and I'm lucky to have you." He remembered the overhead that clinched the match.

"You're so changeable," responded Sonia, "but I suppose you're forgiven."

Charlie admitted she was unerringly accurate. When his game was working well he was a charming person but if his shots were missing their targets he was quite horrible. His mood was dictated by his performance.... on court, that is.

Charlie lashed at the ball as it flew off the back wall. The small yellow dot had taken a great deal of punishment. Charlie had been on court, at his local squash club for a couple of hours, striving for excellence. Nothing short of a faultless length or a precision drop shot would be good enough. If his standard lacked, his personality suffered. He would encourage himself and then turn angry. He would shout abuse at himself, even striking his person with his racket. He knew that if he performed badly, either in a match or a practise session then he would be unhappy, constantly worrying about his ability until he stepped back on a court. Knowing how he would feel fuelled his anger.

Every morning he would arrive early at school to practise as his struggle for superiority was relentless. Every evening Charlie could be seen at the squash club - everything had to be right - nothing else was good enough.

Charlie realised his work was suffering; he was losing ground on the other students. Still, who cares? He was sixth in the county juniors - wasn't that more important than any qualifications? Very few county juniors earn any type of living from their chosen sport so a few examinations might have been very useful but Charlie didn't care. He wanted success on the squash court not in the classroom.

When his peers were studying in the school holidays, Charlie wasn't. Squash tournaments were played through the vacation and these had to take priority.

His first tournament beckoned. Days before the event the nerves were already starting to tingle. This was life and death. If he failed then despondency would hinder any progress. On the other hand success would be fantastic - a platform on which he could build.

Charlie spoke to his friend Justin about the forthcoming event.

"Do you reckon I'll do alright?" Charlie asked his mate, desperately seeking much needed reassurance.

Justin, who had never played in a competitive tournament, was finally able to convince his friend that he would be fine. If we're honest, Justin, short, fat and loyal, knew as much about competitive squash as a monk does about oral sex.

The competition was a county open, a long train ride from where the two boys lived. Charlie and his trusted companion were being given a lift to the station by Charlie's mother.

"I feel sick," moaned Charlie to Justin as they stood by the blue Volvo, "I so badly want to do well. What if I get hammered and look a complete idiot?"

"I'm sure you won't," Justin replied, "you'll be fine. I shouldn't think that many people will have worked as hard as you at their game."

Charlie and his supportive pal, a chap who found friendships difficult to form therefore valued the ones he did have, reached the station with plenty of time to spare. Charlie's mood was forever changing. One minute he would be filled with confidence, a potential great who would grab his chance by the bollocks. Hadn't he worked hard for his chance? In all the films, didn't those who were the most dedicated always succeed? Every spare moment he had struggled with his game, wasn't now the time to reap the rewards? At other intervals he just prayed he wouldn't get hammered and leave the court with pearls of laughter ringing in his ears. You had to have natural ability to win at this level, didn't you?

Ten impressive courts welcomed the duo. Charlie immediately felt intimidated.

"This looks serious," he whispered to Justin. "Everything seems so professional."

"Don't worry," his friend assured him, "you'll be okay."

Soon a few of the first round matches were underway. Charlie walked round, with Justin, looking over the various balconies and viewing the standard on the courts below.

"They're all rather good," said the boy as he watched a tall thin lad dispatch a very accurate drop shot.

Justin didn't utter a sound, but it was obvious to his pal that he was suitably impressed. Charlie knew that if his plumpish chum had any positive comments then he would have made himself heard. His continuing silence didn't inspire confidence.

"Maybe Justin thinks that I'm going to get thrashed" thought Charlie, "but he's too nice to say. I'm glad he came with me, as many of my so-called pals would have enjoyed watching me humiliated. They'd probably have thought that I deserved to look stupid for entering a tournament like this. At least Justin will be genuinely upset for me if I lose."

The rallies on show in this under 16's tournament were played to a good line and length; even the smallest of errors was invariably punished. Charlie grew more and more anxious, praying that his opponent was one of the lesser entrants, or, even better, without the use of every faculty.

"I suppose it will be quite comical if I fail to win a point." He didn't understand the origin of the idea, but it certainly didn't please him.

"Don't be so stupid," he silently rebuked himself. "It will be awful."

"Think positively," he remembered one of his coaches telling him. He tried to - but it wasn't easy.

Eventually Charlie was called to court 4. He was glad the waiting was finally over. Meeting his opponent outside the court he scanned the adversary. He was probably about fifteen years old, a big powerful looking player with fiery red hair. The two contestants walked on court and began the warm-up. Neil, Charlie's opponent, hit the ball hard and accurately.

"You can win this," Charlie encouraged himself; "it will seem a long train journey home if you don't."

The match started equally, with the first four points being evenly distributed. Then Neil, hitting the ball harder than his opponent, established the advantage. Once Charlie conceded the opening game he had to fight to maintain his enthusiasm.

"You won't give up so easily," Charlie reprimanded himself, "this is where it counts. You've worked so bloody hard that you just mustn't lose."

In the real world ability counts for much. Charlie was a dedicated player; Neil a gifted one. A little effort from the bigger lad would go far. Neil won the next two games with comparative ease. It was an extremely dejected Charlie who shook his conqueror's clammy hand.

After suffering heavy and demoralising defeats at the hands of the country's elite juniors, Charlie's obsession with the game diminished, almost as rapidly as it had started. Having given everything to this sport he knew that he had little remaining. Perfection, or even being one of the best, just wouldn't happen. The flame that had burned for so long simply flickered and died. The amount of time and effort already spent didn't upset him, but he wouldn't work at his game anymore. No, he had awoken from the dream and, now, hours practising on court would feel an utter waste. His neurotic attention no longer focused on the physically demanding game of squash. He wasn't one to take pride in a reasonable standard - the best or not at all.

Having already taken his examinations there seemed little point in studying. Why shut the stable door when the horse has bolted? He saw a few schoolmates but all they wanted to discuss was the forthcoming grades and then their next step on life's ladder.

Charlie opened the official looking letter. His heartbeat raced, his hands a little unsteady. If he was honest with himself, he knew he could have tried harder in all areas of academic work.

"Eight 'O' Levels, moderate grades." His mother glared at him. "You didn't even manage an 'A' grade in French."

"If I'd carried on with my dedication to being a scholar," he mused, "I could have done much, much better. I had the ability but not the commitment."

He thought back to all the hours spent on court. He knew that it was something, at the time, he needed to do. His desire to succeed with the racket had been greater than anything else. He wished, at that moment, his introduction to the game had come at a different time.

A few days before the beginning of term, Charlie, with a few other pupils was having a last evening out. They were drinking in a local club, and although the new term hovered threateningly, most of them were enjoying themselves. Charlie had downed three or four pints, then, as is often the way, his mind started to become active. The future worries some, excites others. This topic fuelled the imaginations of Charlie and a fellow pupil as they stood by the bar.

"Do you really want to go back to the sixth form?" asked Paul.

"I don't know," replied Charlie, "my mother was very keen on me returning to do my 'A' levels until my 'O' level results dampened her enthusiasm. Then she realised just because you are at a certain school you can't guarantee automatic success."

"I just find all the studying and the long hours too much," said Paul. "I mean you never have any free time, considering all the week, not forgetting Saturdays, is spent at school. Then you are weighed down with homework. I would like to enjoy myself occasionally, you're only young once."

Charlie nodded his agreement. He considered what his friend had said while he took a sip from his beer glass. He dried his lips with the tatty sleeve of his denim shirt.

"I wonder if I'm thinking straight," Charlie wondered, "but I'm not sure if I'm lazy or just need a change. Will the grass be greener?"

"To be honest with you, Paul, I would rather opt out now and take my chances with finding a half decent career. I mean, to some companies, surely experience is almost as important as qualifications."

"That's quite a good point," commented his pal. "My 'O' level results were quite poor and, if I'm honest with myself, I think that I'd find 'A' levels very difficult. Especially as I am reluctant to make a vast amount of effort. Whereas, it would be very different if I was being paid to do something. Accomplishing any extra skills or qualifications along the way would be an added bonus."

"How many 'O' levels did you pass?" asked Charlie, hoping to hear some results that were worse than his.

"Only five, one B and four C's," answered Paul.

The two boys continued to discuss the problem with both concluding that without pressure from outside parties they would probably reach the same decision. They would quit education and try to make a successful start in the outside world.

"Is it because I really believe that," thought Charlie, "or is it because I no longer have the determination to further my studies. I am no longer obsessive about my work and, maybe, I never had the ability."

Most of the underage drinkers were enjoying the party. Some were laid out on the floor oblivious to their surroundings. The pace had become too much for these inexperienced 'party-animals'.

"I hope that I don't finish tonight in that state," mused Charlie, "you just don't know what will happen."

Other young revellers were dancing madly so they clattered into each other, pushing and shoving. Inevitably, several dancers fell to the ground, and then began the struggle to regain a standing position. Boys were eyeing-up any available talent, nudging each other and laughing.

"Lads' syndrome," mumbled Charlie to nobody in particular, "bit of music, bit of booze and they can take on the world."

Some young bucks who had consumed enough Dutch Courage to make the urge outweigh the fear of rejection were moving from female to female. Drunk, talking rubbish and hardly able to stand, wasn't the response blatantly obvious? Some young studs obviously approached the challenge differently as there were several couples positioned on chairs, stationed around the perimeter of the dance hall. Or could it be that the girls were so paralytic they didn't care about the feeble chat-up lines. One young girl, perhaps fifteen or sixteen, had her skimpy panties in her hand as her tongue darted in and out of a lad's mouth. This chubby specimen had massive ears and a pimple on his hooked nose. A bulge straining against his trousers was becoming increasingly apparent.

"This could be a case of premature ejaculation," Charlie thought, "I hope he has a change of underwear."

At around midnight the dimly lit dance floor was illuminated, signalling no more drinks would be served and guests should start to leave. Eventually people filed towards the door, most looking the worse for wear. Some staggered, holding various objects to maintain an upright stance. Charlie and Paul ambled out together. Charlie felt merry. He wondered if this euphoria was due to the alcohol or having made an important decision about his future.

"I feel good," Charlie thought, "I'm leaving that school and I'm not the only one. So I'm not the only disaster. Now it's up to me."

The following morning Charlie awoke to the sun shining through the gap in his orange curtains. His head pounded as he tried to remember the previous evening. Eventually, it dawned on him. He recalled chatting to Paul and finally the decision he had made.

"I'm sober now and I still reckon that I've made the right decision," he mused.

When Charlie informed his mother she didn't try to hide her disappointment.

"Just because you didn't excel at your 'O' levels doesn't mean you can't achieve good grades in two years, when your 'A' levels come round."

"Look I've made my decision," Charlie insisted, completely out of character for a boy who had a healthy respect for his elders, "I've had enough of full time education. The last three years I've done nothing but study at that school and I want a change. I feel I can achieve something away from tutoring and that's what I intend to do."

His mother experienced several emotions between sadness and anger. She only wanted the best for him, couldn't he see that?

The following Monday, when most of Charlie's school friends were starting the sixth form, he was making his way to the local job centre.

"I am doing the best thing," he tried to convince himself. "I haven't chucked everything away. With my attitude going back to school would have been a waste of time. I'll show everyone I can do it."

For some hours he studied the various positions on offer. Nothing seemed ideal - the better occupations required more qualifications than he'd achieved and the other jobs, being part-time cleaners and waiters and the like, had no prospects.

"There doesn't seem to be much here," Charlie admitted, "I can't go home with nothing, I'll look a complete wally. That would give the Old Dear all the ammunition she needs."

Eventually, as Charlie began to give up any hope of ever finding a worthwhile role, a 'situations vacant' notice grabbed his attention.

Chapter 3

Two weeks later Charlie nervously approached the strongly built wooden door. His first job, this was an important move towards independence.

"If I can make a go of this," Charlie reasoned, "a lot of doors will open. Having some money will make life a lot easier."

A market research position, working for a large, well established company. If everything went as he hoped Charlie could have got a foot on the ladder.

"I really hope that I get on well with the other people who work here," thought Charlie, "I don't want to be an outsider who nobody talks to."

He needn't have worried. They were a great bunch. They all seemed down to earth and soon put the newcomer at ease.

"Well this lot seem okay," thought Charlie. "Should fit in quite well."

That first morning Charlie met Mike. He was a pleasant enough person even though he had suffered some tough knocks in his eventful twenty-three years. A scruffy, perhaps even unhealthy, looking man who had occasionally been on the wrong side of the law and was now trying to start afresh. Charlie found himself very much taken with Mike. He wondered why. You could never be sure where you were. Was he fascinated by the danger? Did the idea of knowing a wrongdoer attract the sheltered young man? Mike and Charlie often spent their breaks in run down cafes discussing their differing pasts and what hopes the future would have in store for them. Charlie had always had food on the table and, within reason, would be handed money when he asked. He wondered what it was like to worry about your next meal and whether you had enough money for the electricity meter.

One cold, sharp winter's morning, Mike and Charlie were having a quick respite during a hard morning's interviewing.

Casually the older man said to the youth, "I've got something in my pocket that I don't want the police to find on me. About eighteen months ago I got a bit of trouble for burglary, so I want to keep clean."

"Bloody hell" thought Charlie, "what have we here?"

Even he found it surprising how excited he had become. Crime intrigued the youth. He found the idea of prison quite awful so, it was possible, he could only feel admiration for somebody who would risk such a terrible fate.

"What is it?" enquired Charlie, trying to keep his voice level.

Now that he was discussing some major robbery or something he certainly didn't want to sound like the local eunuch.

"Blimey." wondered Charlie, "what has Mike got? A stash of drugs or something even worse?"

"It's a knife," Mike whispered, "will you hold on to it for me?"

Charlie stared at his pal. A small, slightly built chap with messy hair and a bad complexion. He found it difficult to imagine his mate in trouble with the law. Nevertheless, he didn't hesitate.

"No problem," he said to his pal, "the plod won't give me a second glance."

"I've got to help him," reasoned Charlie, "it's a tiny risk to help a mate. And I certainly don't want a guy like Mike to think that I'm a wimp."

It did occur to Charlie that if he had refused the request then his friendship with Mike would be at risk. He pushed this idea to the back of his mind. He was being so stupid, wasn't he? Charlie pocketed the weapon and continued with his interviews.

"These people would be horrified if they knew what I was carrying" Charlie smiled to himself, as he politely asked a forty-something woman about her savings.

He felt strangely proud. Wasn't it good to be bad.

"How are you doing, Mike?" asked Charlie, walking beside the older man.

"Not too bad" was the reply, "what about you?"

Charlie, with a need to know, asked, "When you said that you had a bit of trouble about a year and a half ago, what happened?"

Charlie just had to know the extent of crime that was being discussed. Especially, as he was with the offender. He hadn't met many villains and now he was with one he wanted all the details.

"Well" answered Mike, his tone level, certainly not full of pride, "since you ask, it was a while ago and I had borrowed some ready cash from a right nutter. You know, the type of bloke you don't take the piss. I like my bollocks where they are at the moment. I had to borrow the money to keep me in drink. I was too keen on the odd bevy. The thing was, it was more than the occasional pint. I was doing more than twenty quid a day on booze. Anyway matey got a bit funny as I couldn't pay back the money or what he had banged on top. I was a desperate man, I needed funds. Anyway, I broke into a house way out in the country. I triggered the alarm almost immediately, so I had to leg-it. I whipped across the garden and into a field. The coppers, seeing my escape route, surrounded the whole place and then moved in with the dogs."

"This bloke has got some nerve," thought Charlie, not giving a second thought to the intended victims who had come close to losing their hard earned valuables.

"Anyway," continued Mike, "the slags charged me with the offence, but they did give me bail. I went to Crown Court and admitted the job so I could ask for a bit of mercy. Told the judge that it was my first offence and I had been desperate. The judge was a good old boy and he gave me 120 hours community service and two years probation."

After a while, the dynamic duo decided to separate, with the belief that two areas would give them double the amount of interviews.

"I'm starving," Charlie moaned aloud, "either somebody has cut my throat or it's past my lunch time."

He wandered around until he found a welcoming shop - fish and chips were on the menu.

"Cod and chips, mate, please," Charlie said.

Having paid for his cuisine Charlie left the shop and ambled slowly down the road, munching his edibles. Finishing his tasty tucker, Charlie drop kicked the empty wrapper over somebody's gate. He turned to go and retrieve the litter, and then stopped.

"Bloody-hell" he thought, "my mate is a hardened burglar and I'm shitting myself about dropping a bit of rubbish."

His hands felt greasy so when he passed a public lavatory he opted to give them a quick wash. Shaking the last few drops of icy water from his hands Charlie turned round. It was then he first noticed the two large, black males standing in the toilet's doorway.

"This isn't right," panicked Charlie, adrenaline pumping through his body.

Before he had time to further his thoughts the men were next to him. One to the front and the other to the side. Charlie remembered his first day at school. The unknown always holds a reason for fear. He saw himself wandering through the massive doors, just not sure. His first visit to the headmaster - a terrified lad of four. He had pissed himself then; the fear was as great now, could it be even worse? The moment hung in the grimy air. It was as if Charlie had knocked on the door and awaited the headmaster's response. A child's fear transferred to the adult world. Charlie's mind raced continually but reached nothing to help.

"Were they going to rob him or worse?"

He recalled sitting with his posh pals from senior school watching certain programmes. The news - some poor sod had been mugged or shot. That didn't happen to people like them. They came from a privileged world - crime didn't happen to snobs. For some reason he remembered Jaws. He had seen it with Toby.

"Would you go and help a friend if he was attacked by a shark like that?" Toby had questioned.

"I would like to think so" was the reply, "but maybe I'm not a hero."

At the moment, being a hero was far from Charlie's thoughts. His heart was beating so furiously, he worried it would burst through his chest. As the monster at the front unzipped his stained green trousers, the man to the side pushed the terrified youth forcibly to his knees.

"Am I gay," thoughts rushed into Charlie's brain. "When people blew kisses at me in class maybe they knew something I didn't."

Charlie's body was numb. This hideous nightmare was happening to somebody else - wasn't it? He couldn't struggle. He didn't scream. He was a young lad lying in the dark bedroom, scared of the bogeyman but too scared to cry for fear of being heard. A time of crisis and he was found wanting. He was desperate for an intervention. Would someone run into his private hell and rescue him? They would if he was on television. Charlie was in the grip of terror. It appeared that this thing had got inside him and frozen his ability to function.

25

"I've taken so much for granted" Charlie stifled a sob, "doing what I want, when I want, with my own body."

Charlie's shaky hand touched something. Even with so many hormones pumping through his person, he realised what it was. Mike's knife. Very gradually Charlie started to relax. He didn't feel calm, far from it. He did, nevertheless, sense a feeling of hope. His heartbeat slowed and some feeling returned to his extremities.

"He was going to stand-up for himself. Yes, he could prove himself. Maybe, he would be like Mike. Imagine that."

"You're gonna love this, you white bitch," growled the beast at the front.

Charlie tightened his grip on the weapon. He heard somebody, from somewhere, probably within, utter "you in all, you fucking bastard."

"Was this really him," flashed across his mind, he had never been aggressive, scared even. Crime fascinated, even impressed him. What the hell had he done? Couldn't he have waved the knife in the air and ran? Could he have got away? Did he do the right thing?"

The knife came out and embedded itself in the assailant's stomach. Time froze.

"This proves I'm no prat." Charlie tried to unravel his mind. "When people took the piss I'd laugh it off. Now I know that wasn't because I was afraid - just fair."

Everything happened at once. Blood, emotions flowed freely. Life reached the lowest and highest points, together.

The two women, each pushing a pram, laughed and joked. Charlie noticed them as he staggered out of the toilet's graffiti-covered exit. He didn't glance back, he just kept going.

"Don't look" he whimpered to himself, "I mustn't see those two bastards, whatever state they're in. If they're following.... oh God, I hope not."

He wanted to run. He thought his legs were working - they must have been as he was no longer near the toilets. He prayed that he would find his way home. He couldn't picture his route, but he seemed to go the right way. He recalled the attention of a smartly dressed city gent.

"Did he know what had happened? He couldn't - could he? Was it written on his face? No, he was being paranoid. Understandable, under the circumstances."

Little else of his return journey could be recalled. It was like a horrible dream - pieces are invariably missing when the sleeper awakes.

The next few days passed in a trance. Charlie attempted the motions of life but everything seemed to be happening to this other person. This other person, outwardly, appeared to be coping. Well, if he could cope with a pair of perverts in a grotty toilet then, surely eating and washing would not be a challenge.

During the next few weeks, Charlie tried to regain some sort of normality.

"I won't let them get to me," he urged himself, "I mean, for God's sake, nothing happened! I didn't do anything wrong - I was just bloody unlucky. And it was lucky that I had the knife; I mean, what choice did I have? Anyone would react in the same way."

His main problems occurred at night as he tried to fall asleep. As he shut his eyes, the bastards would appear. Their features would be perceived with such clarity, he would find himself drenched in perspiration. His heart would pound with such ferocity, he was astounded the noise failed to disturb his sister snoring in the adjacent bedroom.

"Surely, it should have been her and not me," he sobbed inwardly, rape - a bloke? I've heard of it but never in a million years......."

Invariably, Charlie would be forced to switch on the bedside light. Then he would lie in the illuminated room and try to focus his mind on more pleasant matters. He would remember a good joke he had heard during the day. Well, it would have been good if his mind hadn't been elsewhere. The vermin in the toilet obsessed him; they seemed to be able to enter his mind at will. He would spend hours reading light-hearted material, but as he read the words, blurred by his tears, he could think of one, and only one, event. Usually, as the birds were starting to sing in the trees, sleep would finally come to his rescue. Even then the torture didn't end. Night terrors were frequent, appearing to become more realistic. At times Charlie even imagined that he could smell his attackers' stink.

"Oh no, I can feel, smell and see them. What would they have done to me? Would they have let me live?" Charlie failed in his attempt to remain calm.

During his waking hours, Charlie was a different person. He was jumpy and offhand with everyone, whether they deserved it or not.

"I wish I wasn't behaving like this," Charlie thought after yelling at his sister, "but what can I do? I know that I'm behaving badly and I know why; the problem being, what can I do to stop it?"

His observant mother noticed he had undergone a personality change, obviously not knowing why. He was permanently tired due to lack of sleep and had no enthusiasm for everyday life. Another monotonous afternoon and Charlie sat in front of the television.

"Just got to find something to occupy my mind," he mumbled.

He was flicking through the channels, when a random programme caught his attention. He didn't really understand why. The bulletin showed a reconstruction of the mugging of a frail old lady. Then the victim was pictured in hospital. These pictures bothered Charlie very much..... very, very much.

"Wouldn't it be terrible to do something like that to a defenceless old woman?" Charlie said to himself.

This was stating the obvious but for Charlie the rest of his life had begun. Obsessive behaviour was, once again, about to control part of the sufferer's life.

Inevitably, night followed day. Nonetheless for Charlie a new fixation had grown in his muddled mind.

"I won't ever hurt an old lady," he constantly reassured himself. "I will avoid them at all times and if I'm in a public place I'll keep a check on my hands. I certainly won't swing my arms about without checking first..... I mean, you can't be too careful."

The young man was totally preoccupied with his behaviour. Whenever he went out on encountering an old lady evasive action would be taken. He was desperate to keep the promise he had made himself - he would avoid female pensioners at all costs. Most people have a healthy respect for pensioners and would, consequently be worried about harming them. Charlie's concerns were so magnified he worried obsessively that he would commit a malicious act directed at one of them. A slight amount of anxiety is the norm;

however such a vast degree, which inhibits thought and disrupts normal everyday activities, is a desperate problem.

"What am I gonna do?" Charlie panicked, as yet again his obsessions created havoc. "Am I just a born worrier or is something badly wrong with me? I can't cope with this shit."

As the days passed his obsessions showed no sign of leaving him. He had to admit his mental state was deteriorating.

A sunny Tuesday Charlie, impressed by the weather, decided to walk down the local village to buy a newspaper. He strolled down a country lane that took him to the village.

"This is nice," he mused, more relaxed than usual.

The calm before the storm.

Approaching him on the same side of the quiet road was an elderly couple. Charlie guessed they were both probably in their late seventies or early eighties. The gentleman walked with a limp and the lady was bent forward giving the impression that she suffered with her back. As the elderly female had an escort, Charlie didn't cross the road to avoid her but carried on towards the dithering duo.

"Should be okay," Charlie tried to convince himself, "I'll make sure that the old boy is between me and the old girl."

Charlie marched past quickly, holding his hands together to ensure he didn't strike either one. He paced onwards and it was then the doubts started.

"Did I hit her?" he wondered anxiously.

He looked round to check the welfare of the elderly couple.

"They're fine," he assured himself, "nothing happened. I swear, nothing happened."

His words of wisdom fell on deaf ears. Not so much deaf as disbelieving. Unable to believe. He knew, that is to say he would have staked his sister's life, that he hadn't struck either of the elderly pedestrians, but actually convincing himself, well, that was quite a different matter. The disturbed young man found this difficult, practically impossible. To a normal thinking person the situation would not have posed any discomfort, but to Charlie it was an entirely different scenario.

"What if I'm responsible for injury to one of those oldies?" Charlie's mind was in a whirl.

"Don't be such a wanker," he reasoned, "If you'd have hit them they'd have bloody noticed - wouldn't they?"

The incident continued to bother him. While he mentally replayed the events of passing the couple, time and again, he felt his control slipping from him.

"Calm down, for fuck's sake get a grip" his voice heightened in panic.

His heartbeat increased and a stabbing pain developed in his chest.

"Shit," he thought, "I hope this isn't the end. I must get control."

After a short period, which seemed an eternity, Charlie began to take control of his bodily functions. Nevertheless, the start of a headache made it hard for the young man to concentrate on anything but the incident. He wiped the beads of perspiration, formed on his forehead, with a shaky hand and turned for home. He really could not have cared what was happening in the world - forget the newspaper, he had other concerns. Back home Charlie flopped in a cushioned chair and considered the because of his anxiety. Time and again, that moment when he passed the old couple was replayed in his mind. As time passed he grew easier about the situation, he would eventually relax until, of course, the next incident occurred.

"I'm not going to go out alone," Charlie thought, one sunny weekend. "I know that I'll spend the entire time shitting myself about meeting an old dear."

Later in the week he phoned a friend and decided to venture out with an escort.

"Now, I've got somebody to check my actions. If I hit an old biddy they'll probably mention it." He tried to maintain a sense of humour.

Later, inside a month, Charlie found it really difficult to leave the house at all, accompanied or not. "If I did clump somebody," he mused, "it would be too late. What could anyone be expected to do?"

So he dwelt at his mother's abode totally in fear of his obsession. Thoughts, some old, others new, whirled around in his head. Was he mad? Did other people have similar problems? Was he weak? Why couldn't he live normally in society? Would these thoughts ruin his whole life?

As he sat in his bedroom day after day, he grew lonely, frightened and depressed. "I'm trapped" he sniffed loudly, "somewhere very unpleasant. If I think about my problems they just seem to get ten times worse. There isn't any escape. Maybe, it would be better if I could tell someone."

A miserable Wednesday, with rain against the window and wind howling in the trees, the young man felt angry. The death of his beloved cat, Poppy, did not help his darkening mood.

"I must deserve all this bollocks," he cursed, "I must have done something fucking bad."

The following day the anger was replaced by sadness.

"Why me? Am I such a nasty, horrible person? All I want to do is feel and act normally."

He decided, quite logically, that to become a normal human he required an environment that lacked one ingredient - old women.

"If they're not there, you can't mug them," Charlie thought to himself.

Happy with the belief that he could roam the deserted streets at night without a realistic chance of encountering a pensioner an idea began to hatch in his brain.

Chapter 4

"Hi ya Rob, it's me Charlie. How ya been?" Charlie spoke softly into the receiver.

"Not bad mate," answered Rob, sounding quite pleased to hear from an old pal.

"Well, this is okay," mused Charlie, "I'm glad that Rob seems okay. I was a plonker to worry about his reaction to my call."

"So what's been going on?" continued Charlie aloud, "how's Kate? Have you seen anyone else?"

Kate was Rob's sister. They were a peculiar pair; she being tall and heavily built with dark hair and he of slim physique, fairly short and blonde.

"Kate's okay," replied Rob, "still ain't doing a lot by way of finding a job. A bit of baby-sitting and that's about it."

"What about you?" Charlie asked.

"I lost my job at the printer's. Now I do a bit of labouring on a few local sites. How's that pal of yours, Jane?" Rob changed the subject.

"Same as ever," replied Charlie, "still working in the same place, driving the same car and bossing me about."

"She's been a good pal to me," thought Charlie. "Sometimes I don't know how I would have coped without her. Driving me about, lending me money, the list goes on and on..... how the hell would I have managed?"

Rob agreed to go round and see Charlie and Jane as the time had ticked away but the conversation had not dried-up. It's amazing how gossip fills the hours.

"Is it okay if I bring Kate?" asked Rob.

"Yeah no problem, mate," Charlie replied. "See you later."

"I hope their visit goes well" Charlie mused, having replaced the receiver, "it would be really good to have a couple of people on my side."

One evening, a few days later, Charlie, Rob, Kate and Jane sat round the long, white kitchen table.

"I need to direct the chatter," Charlie thought, "got to find out the circumstances before I blunder along with any plans."

"I tell you something" Charlie sighed, "I haven't a penny to call my own."

"Well at least you're not in as much debt as I am" interrupted Rob, "when I had my last job, I borrowed everything I could, not to mention living in sin with my flexible friends. I owe thousands. And to be honest, the money those bastards pay me at the moment, I ain't gonna pay much of it back."

"Snap." said Kate. "I hate the idea of a full-time job. Okay, I do get a few quid for looking after people's kids but I love a night at the pub. Nowadays, you buy a round and that's all your money. I'd just love to have enough money to do what I want, when I want."

"This was perfect," thought Charlie, a couple of dossers - no money, little income, hate working. Fantastic - neither of them had anything to lose."

Charlie glanced at Jane.

"I'm sure she'd go for it," he thought, "anything for a buzz. Anyway, she's such a loyal mate that I reckon she would do it so as not to let me down."

"We could always do a job" smiled Charlie. He tried to mask his intent to guide the group to his idea with a cheeky grin. He'd just considered this suggestion; he certainly didn't want his crowd to think that he'd planned this moment since the telephone conversation.

The other three looked at each other. Nervous smiles, looking like children who were about to relate a rude joke - their parents may not approve. Hair was flicked from faces - another sign of nervous contemplation. None of the group was horrified - they certainly didn't see the idea as a moral dilemma.

"Not too bad," reasoned Charlie, "with a bit of work I could have this lot robbing banks."

Charlie, long before, had concluded that the answer to his prayers was prison. Strange, you may think, but there was a method in his madness.

"No old dears in there," he had told himself.

"Also," he thought, "a lot of crimes can be committed at night so I won't have to risk hitting some old woman while I am breaking the law. I mean I'm not very likely to meet someone's granny at one o'clock in the morning going for a stroll."

So the young man had decided to try and earn some money at night - stealing. The risk of capture didn't worry him in the least. If he were sent to prison he would be cured. His neurotic thoughts would no longer pose a problem. That punishment would be Heaven sent, not much of a deterrent. The powers of persuasion are a wonderful thing. Soon the three visitors were totally convinced that a life of crime would be enjoyable, not to mention profitable.

"Marvellous," thought Charlie, "that was really easy. I even nearly convinced myself that I've no other reason except personal gain and, of course, to have a superb time."

Charlie certainly wasn't going to let the grass grow. It would be nothing short of tragic if any of the others changed their minds.

Just three days and events were taking place.

"Pass me the screwdriver, Rob," whispered Charlie.

"This is the life," Charlie tried to convince himself, "it doesn't get much better than this."

"You sad fucker," Charlie silently contradicted himself, "if this is the best it gets..... God help us."

"Some people have to settle for less than others," millions of thoughts filled Charlie's head in a fraction of a second. "With my problem I'm not gonna set the world on fire. I just have to make the most of what I've got. I mean, we can't all have birds with slim hips and big tits."

The two girls were parked a little way down the road in Jane's car. Charlie determined this was the best way to avoid having the registration plates taken.

"Why did he want to avoid capture, surely that was the most important part of his master plan?" he questioned himself.

He pictured the look of horror and disgust on his mother's face. Her son, privately educated.... hell, what did he think he was doing taking from others?

"I reckon that would be the worst part of being nicked," Charlie thought, "Hazel would be a nightmare. I don't know if she'd give me the silent treatment or rant and rave. Maybe, tears.... oh fuck. Still, I'll probably be inside so it won't matter. By the time I get out she'll have got over it."

Charlie felt terrible. Often he would try and act like a ruthless thug but beneath the hard exterior was a kindly, if somewhat muddled, young man.

"What the bloody hell am I supposed to do?" Charlie asked himself. "Take Hazel to one side and tell her I am turning to crime because I want to go to prison. When she asks why I want to lose my freedom I'm sure she'll understand completely when I say that I don't want to be near any old women as I'm scared I'll beat them about. I mean... Christ... live a bit."

Rob transferred the long thin metal object to Charlie, who grasped it with a trembling hand. Was it nerves or anticipation? His anger, directed inwards, killed any nerves. At times, he felt that owing to circumstances he was doing a good and generous act. If he were caught a cure for his problem would be forthcoming. That was good for society as well as himself, wasn't it?

To Charlie's surprise the window jolted open with comparative ease.

"Magic," he thought, "so far so good."

The dishonest duo entered the building trying to be as quick and quiet as possible. They looked around shining the torch.

"This is it," Charlie thought. "I've done an offence. Now I've started I might as well carry on. In for a penny, in for a pound."

Suddenly Rob grabbed Charlie's arm nearly causing the amateur felon to shriek aloud. What was it? Was somebody outside?

"Shit," panicked Charlie, "this could be all over before it's began. Kids of nine and ten do hundreds of burglaries - I can't even manage one."

"Look over there," squeaked Rob, seemingly on the point of orgasm, "it's a television and video recorder."

"I must stop thinking the worst," Charlie told himself as his pulse slowed, "I must think positive."

Charlie darted across the darkened room, closely followed by his mate. He grabbed the twenty-four inch television, only to discover that it was screwed to a wall bracket. A quick glance at the video revealed this was also secure.

"Shit," muttered Charlie, "what now?"

"Don't worry," said Robert, "we've got two screwdrivers, it should be quite easy to sort it. Come on, it shouldn't take long."

With their hands shaking the two intruders set about their task. After what seemed like an eternity, Rob whispered, "I've done the first screw. How are you getting on?"

"Not bad," was the reply, "nearly there."

"I reckon I've left my stomach at the window" Charlie mused.

"It doesn't matter a toss if you're nicked" the thief reminded himself, "then you'll be better. Free of these thoughts."

"Yeah, I guess," Charlie continued the conversation in his head, "but I've decided to do this job and now I want to get away with it. I just can't get myself arrested on purpose. Anyway, I don't want to be a failure at everything I do."

Eventually, after about five minutes, which seemed more like five hours, the electronic equipment was ready to remove. They loaded it through the window and carried it to the car.

"There wasn't anybody about, was there, Rob?" questioned Charlie as they approached the vehicle.

"Nothing, mate," puffed Rob, "we've got away with that one."

"That's great." enthused Charlie.

"I'm fucked," replied Rob.

"At least I'm not a complete wally," thought Charlie, "I'm glad that I can do something right. Once I'd started the job I just had to get away with it. I suppose I would be okay in prison so I'll keep on nicking but, for now, I'll give my best at what I've decided to do - legal or not."

"Get your head straight," he silently reprimanded himself.

"All I'm saying," he answered the unspoken query, "I will steal until I get put away. While I am stealing I'll do my best to earn money and be a good thief."

"What a terrific guy, you are." Charlie mocked himself.

Charlie returned to reality as he opened the door of their getaway car.

"Brilliant," enthused Kate when she saw their haul, "that's really good."

The foursome, complete with their ill-gotten gains, drove off.

Charlie locked the garden shed.

"We'll have to try and find somebody who'll buy 'em off us," he told Rob, "do you know anyone?"

"Now we've gone to all this trouble, I want to get something out of it," reasoned Charlie, "no point doing all that for nothing. I know that the others are expecting loads of dosh."

"I'll ask about," his pal agreed.

So there it was. Four rebels and a car. A life of criminal success or a major error? Rebelling against what or whom? Most nights they would steal car stereos and when it was late enough commit a burglary. They never burgled houses. Charlie told the others that it was unfair to rob directly from people.

"How would you feel if you came home and some shit had nicked all your valuables? Not to mention wrecking your place," he challenged them.

"Gutted," admitted Rob.

The ladies agreed.

"Also," Charlie thought inwardly, "what the hell would I do if I came across an old dear while I was in some house? I wouldn't end up in prison, more like bloody hospital." He decided not to share these thoughts with his partners.

Confidence grew as the nights of crime continued. Some of the escapades remained clearly in the confused mind of the instigator. The group always thieved away from home, Charlie insisted.

"It ain't a good idea to shit on your own doorstep," he informed the troops.

"Don't want to rob someone who knows me," he silently considered, "might get some nutter at my house with the hump. "He didn't voice these private concerns as he certainly didn't want the others to think that he might be scared.

One chilled night, a multi-storey car park, the penultimate floor. The gang found rows of parked cars.

"There is a night-club down the road," Charlie told the others, "this lot are probably trying to get their nuts wet on the dance floor."

"Well they'll get more than they bargained for," added Rob, "some of them will lose more than their virginity."

Kate climbed from their car and checked the area, you couldn't be too careful. Finally, she gave the two men the thumbs-up. Having checked the first vehicle for an alarm, Charlie, using a small screwdriver, popped the side window. Quiet but effective. Rob finished the job. Even Charlie admitted he was very good at removing a stereo without causing damage. Each unprotected car had similar treatment. After everything was sorted the goods were taken to Charlie's shed. The group did not want to drive around with stolen property in their car. That would be very stupid. As time allowed, the group moved to another car park. People would always be daft enough to leave a car unattended at night. It was about two o'clock in the morning, late enough for a burglary. The target was already sorted. The two lads left the girls in the car and crept quietly down a dark narrow alley. They arrived at the back door of a newsagents' shop.

"I've done loads of jobs," thought Charlie, "yet I shit myself more each time. I suppose that the longer you get away with it, the higher the stakes. I do still reckon prison would be a blessing in disguise but I really do want to be good at something. Thieving or science, at least I'm good at something."

The flimsy door didn't delay the two bandits for very long. To be honest that door wouldn't have deterred a determined stray dog.

"People aren't very wary of crime," reasoned Charlie, "a gust of wind and that door would be at the end of the road."

The two lads ran into the front of the shop with Rob holding open a bin liner. The alarm sounded, screeching through the cold night air.

"I'm surprised the alarm works," Charlie smiled to himself, "the rest of the security is a joke."

Charlie threw as many cigarettes into the bin liner as he could. The amount surprised even him. It's amazing what a bucket load of adrenaline can achieve.

"Now I can see why athletes always achieve their best times in the big races." Charlie thought.

Isn't it strange what goes through your mind when the pressure is on? Three minutes passed in a whirl - time to go.

"That's the mistake a lot of thieves make," thought Charlie as the duo departed, "they get greedy. It would have been so easy to stay in the shop and keep grabbing."

They returned to their vehicle and then, slowly, the car pulled away. Once the four were confident of their success, excited chatter filled the vehicle.

One rainy night, later the same week, the group were all sitting in Jane's trusty vehicle deciding what to do.

"Well, I need some tyres for my car," offered Rob, "and as there are plenty of cars about, with perfect wheels, I thought..."

"Why not?" answered Charlie.

"Actually," continued Rob, "there is a garage forecourt just along the road."

"Sounds okay," said Charlie, not wanting to let down a friend.

The female duo parked as near as they could, obviously not wanting to be noticed.

Rob and Charlie were soon at work. When the lads left the vehicle stood on a pile of bricks.

Mid morning, the following day, Rob arrived at his friend's abode. The door was unlocked but there was no answer.

"Sister Lucy and mummy Hazel must have gone to work" thought Rob, "and Charlie is still in bed. Lazy fucker."

Rob strolled through the spacious kitchen and, as expected, found his chum snuggled in his divan.

"Come on Chaz," said the visitor, "it's almost midday."

Charlie opened his eyes and peered at Rob, the light causing him to squint. He covered his shaven head with the luminous pink duvet.

"Suppose I'd better get up," he thought. "Love to stay in bed all day but there are jobs to be planned and coffee to be drunk."

"Alright mate," he mumbled, "I'll just throw on some clothes."

Charlie pulled on an old tee shirt and a baggy pair of denim dungarees. Fashion model of the year - he wasn't.

"I'm a scruffy git," he reflected, "never gonna pull a nice tart."

"With your problems," he silently reminded himself, "being scruffy is the least of your worries. Why should anyone want a nice girl when they want to go to jail just to feel normal?"

Charlie struggled into the kitchen and almost fell onto an available chair. Rob flicked the switch on the kettle. Charlie could almost taste the coffee.

"Good result last night," began Rob.

"Yeah, reckon we've got luck on our side," replied Charlie, "and they say that crime doesn't pay. I think we should try for bigger and better things."

"What, you mean, riskier jobs?" said Rob.

"Well yeah," replied his mate. "I mean the worst they can do is lock us up. We could nick a car and drive it through a shop window. When you've got a stolen car you have a lot more options."

Charlie really had lost the plot.

"It's not that I need the money," Charlie mused, "but the higher the risk, the greater chance of prison. My irrational thoughts are getting worse by the day and I need to do something. If we aren't getting nicked on the little jobs then I reckon I should try something bigger. I mean, some days I can't leave the bloody house 'til it is dark as the thoughts are so bad. The only time I go out is to thieve. If I got caught, well... it might be problem solved. When I get out of nick the thoughts might have gone and I can live a bit."

Rob, it has to be said, didn't look thrilled at the idea of a long spell behind bars.

"Probably worried about getting his botty felt in the showers," Charlie smiled to himself.

The kettle clicked. The caffeine stimulated Charlie's mind. The start of another disturbing day.

"How's Kate this morning?" asked Charlie.

"Not sure. I doubt if she's fallen out of bed yet," was the reply.

Leaving their dirty mugs on the table the duo went out into the large back garden. Charlie grabbed the leather football from the shed and launched it towards his friend. Two cricket stumps formed the goal. Charlie took his place between the posts and the game began. Rob chipped the ball from the right side of the lawn. Charlie dived and tipped the ball over the imaginary crossbar.

"I feel good," he thought, "I do love this game. It doesn't matter if it is a knockabout or a serious match."

Charlie caught Rob's next effort.

"One good thing about being in goal in such a wide open space," reasoned Charlie, "is the lack of horrible thoughts. I can see for miles so if I do worry that I've struck an old lady it is easy to check.

Anyway, if my mind really gives me trouble I can ask Rob. He might not be England standard at footie but I'm sure he would know if some old dear ran across the pitch."

After a while the two lads were exhausted. They staggered to the kitchen and gulped two more drinks - just what the doctor ordered.

"Was anyone by the door when we came in?" Charlie asked Rob.

"No mate, why?" Rob sounded surprised.

"Sorry, must be going potty," Charlie laughed, "but you are sure?"

"Bloody certain," Rob replied.

Charlie was happy. He had checked his latest worry. The two pals lazed in the kitchen drinking and chatting for the best part of the afternoon.

"What we really need," said Rob, "is an easy job that will give us a lot of money."

"That would be nice," answered Charlie, who didn't really care if there was a high risk factor or not.

The two men were surprised a little later when Jane appeared.

"Afternoon's holiday," she informed her two pals.

Once again they discussed their illegal activities.

"I believe," commented Jane, "with a bit of good fortune and without taking too many risks that we can keep going for ages."

A little later Charlie dialled Kate's phone number.

"Hello Kate," he said, "are you coming round? Jane and Rob are here."

"Alright then," replied Kate, "give me a minute and I'll be with you. Are Hazel or Lucy about?"

"No, don't worry," answered Charlie, "they're both out so we can discuss business."

It wasn't long before the foursome was settled around the kitchen table, each sipping a hot drink.

"Well, what about tonight," began Jane, "any ideas?"

"Well," answered Rob, not giving anyone else a chance to speak, "I reckon we should stick to the usual routine. Leave here about ten o'clock, collect as many stereos as possible 'til the early hours and then case a couple of joints that might be worth a spin."

"He definitely doesn't want to do anything bigger," reasoned Charlie, "still why should he? He's earning a bit of money, having a laugh, so why would he want to go to prison? It's not as if he's got to cope with a fucked thought pattern. I wonder if the idea of jail scares him? He's a mouthy little bloke so he probably would get plenty of slaps."

Charlie glanced at the two girls.

"I don't think they want to risk anything else," Charlie continued. "I'm sure that neither of them would like to go down for a day so I doubt they'd enjoy a couple of years."

Charlie stared out of the window.

"I suppose that we are all in this for different reasons," he mused, "I'm trying to cope with my mind and I believe prison would help. The others want a good time and extra cash. Even if they were nicked I'm sure they'd try and avoid a stint in custody. Then again, what normal person wouldn't?"

The gang agreed on some suitable dishonest toil. With this matter sorted the conversation turned to the previous night.

"What do you reckon those poor sods will think when they see their cars? They'll be gutted," laughed Rob.

"I reckon that Rob enjoys upsetting people more than he likes the money and the buzz." thought Charlie. "Still, I suppose his life is shit so he likes to think of other people in a mess. At least I've got an excuse for my behaviour. I do feel quite bad about leaving some poor bastard without a car stereo or a social club without a television. If it wasn't for these bastard thoughts I'd like to think I could lead a good life. Then again, I do have to admit that I did take Rob and the others down this road. I just didn't expect Rob to enjoy giving other people the hump….. not quite so much, anyway.

It was just after nine when Jane said to her companions, "shall we have one last cuppa then make a move?"

They all agreed. After finishing their drinks they began to equip themselves - a pair of gloves per person and a screwdriver apiece for the two males. And, of course, nobody could forget Percy, their trusty crowbar. They loaded their vehicle and, chattering nervously, sped towards the first car park.

"Will tonight be the night," Charlie pondered, "could something break? We've all become really confident over the last few weeks, could that be our downfall? Maybe I'll find out really soon if prison will sort out my screwed-up head. Things have got bad lately with shitty thoughts so I really couldn't care if prison was only a car stereo away."

He glanced at the others. "Would they be so keen to follow my lead if they knew what was going round inside my head? Somehow, I doubt it."

"You alright Chaz?" Rob's squeaky voice interrupted Charlie's concerns.

"Fine mate," Charlie replied, "I reckon we'll do well tonight, I feel bloody lucky."

Chapter 5

Early one summer's morning Charlie was awoken by a car stopping outside his house.

"What the fuck is that?" Charlie wondered if he was dreaming.

As he got nearer to the land of consciousness he realised that visitors were unexpected at this hour; not to mention, bloody unwelcome. Adrenaline started to pump through his person. Soon, he was fully awake. He peeped through his curtains and there they were. Three patrol cars. The adrenaline that had started a few seconds earlier now threatened to leave the young man in a state of collapse.

"Fucking hell." murmured Charlie, "this is not quite what I had in mind. I should have expected this but, I don't know, my bloody parents are here. What the hell are they going to make of this little lot?"

Charlie, clad in his boxer shorts and ripped T-shirt, hurriedly left the house.

"I must get out there before the old girl and the old boy," he panicked, "don't want them talking to the police."

Two bulky officers of the law approached him.

"Are you Charlie Lloyd?" one of them asked.

"That's right," replied Charlie.

"Then I'm arresting you for burglary and theft. You have the right to remain silent, but what you do say, can and will be used against you in a court of law."

Charlie's parents, having come out to witness the scene, looked horrified. Charlie could feel their eyes drilling into the back of his head.

"Thank God the plod are here," Charlie mused. "I reckon the old biddy would happily push me off a cliff. She must be gutted. Her pride and joy being marched away by the police."

Charlie didn't have a clue what to say. Trying to say sorry just didn't seem adequate. He had taken everything they had done for him and, without a word of thanks, spat it back. There was only one answer for a scared, confused, wannabe master villain - false bravado.

Charlie sauntered to his bedroom, avoiding the glare from his parents.

"Keep calm," he urged himself, "in a few years we'll all have a good laugh about this."

Meanwhile, his father placed a comforting arm on his mum's shoulder. It was obvious that she was close to tears.

A confused young man, dressed as he felt inside - an utter mess, returned to the vehicles and, silently, clambered into the nearest one.

The policemen were laughing and joking *en route* to the local station.

"I wonder why they're acting like we are mates," thought Charlie, "I suppose it's easier for them if we can get on."

"That Rob's a bit of a wanker," chuckled one of the officers, "he only went back to the garage where you two nicked the tyres to fill-up with petrol. Even that numb-nut attendant realised the wheels were stolen."

At the station a terrified Rob, unsure of the *modus operandi*, had named names - Kate and Charlie, to be exact. It dawned on Charlie that darling Rob had, not content with the wheels, told the police about the bloody lot. The only aspect that he had decided not to mention was Jane's involvement.

"Probably wants to give her one," Charlie thought. He had often wondered if the pair were more than pals.

"What a prick." Charlie's mind wandered to more important issues, "how could someone go back to a place they'd robbed with the stuff they'd nicked."

"So Charlie, have you got anything to tell us?" said the detective constable, staring at the anxious youth across the interview room.

"Well, I suppose this is what I planned" Charlie thought to himself. "I do feel bad, really bad, about upsetting all the people I robbed but what else could I do? I've got this bloody curse so I didn't have any choice. Surely, it is better that I get myself nicked for pinching a few bits and pieces than beating some old dear. I mean, if I hadn't got nicked I could have ended-up doing some serious damage to an old woman."

He tried to convince himself that he was doing society a favour.

"If this is what it takes to stop myself, then I'll just have to live with it," he told himself. "I must admit I do wish I could explain my problem to my mum - she really did look gutted."

After several cigarettes, cups of coffee and probing questions, Charlie confessed his sins. He was shown the statements made by Rob and Kate and knew he was doomed.

"Fuckers," he thought, "what happened to honour among thieves? I don't mind going to prison but I thought they were better pals than that."

For a while he sat in the interview room and wondered if he blatantly denied everything, would they be able to charge him. Now prison seemed so very close he wondered if there was any alternative escape from his warped mind.

"They found nicked gear at home," he remembered, "let's face it - the only cure you could suggest will be tested - probably sooner rather than later."

Charlie started to talk. He told the officers what they wanted to hear but he was careful, very careful, not to mention any names. He explained why certain vehicles had been targeted owing to their location and how he had forced entry to numerous properties.

The police were thorough; they wanted every detail, leaving no stone unturned.

"So," continued the detective constable, "tell us about the gymnasium. Robert said that you and he did that together while Kate stayed in the car, down the road."

Charlie recalled this burglary with ease. It had felt good. He had felt like a professional. They would never get him. Soon the crown jewels would be stashed in his shed.

"Well," started the prisoner, wondering why he kept staring at the constable's eyes, "we hopped out the car and crept to the building. All the doors were locked and the windows were out of reach so we had a problem. Anyway, on the far side, we found a shed. The roof was flat and it looked quite easy to reach. From there we could get to the windows of the gym."

Charlie was suddenly distracted.

"He's got a squint," he realised as he stared at the constable. "I knew that there was something strange about his eyes."

"Carry on," said Squint, making Charlie focus on reality.

"Rob gave me a hand and I struggled onto the roof" Charlie continued, "and from here it was easy to reach the windows. I always

46

kept my screwdriver in my dungarees so opening the window was a doodle."

"What then?" asked the detective sergeant, a fat man in his late forties.

"Well," answered Charlie, "all I had to do was reach the floor. Anyway, near the window were some wall bars. These had ropes attached to them so my prayers were answered."

"Then what?" questioned Squint.

"I wonder if he's looking at me," thought Charlie, "I can't really be sure."

"Well, I had a quick look round the building," Charlie spoke aloud, "to see what was worth taking. I nipped over to the fruit machine and forced the back panel. I emptied each tube into a plastic bag that I had brought with me. I reckon I took about a hundred quid. Then I had a go at the drinks machine. That had about seventy pounds in it. At least, it did until I arrived."

"Don't try and be funny," interrupted Porky. "Hasn't it occurred to you that you're in deep trouble? Thieving is wrong, or didn't you know?"

"So is eating too much," Charlie thought to himself, "but that doesn't seem to worry you."

Aloud, the offender continued, "I couldn't find anything else worth taking so I crept to the front door. It was easy to open from the inside. I went and found Rob and, then, we made our way to the car."

"That seems to tie in quite nicely with Rob's and Kate's accounts," commented Squint.

The interview dragged on. An hour or more passed and, finally, Squint and Porky were satisfied with the prisoner's statement. Charlie was returned to his cell.

"What would happen to the trio now?" Charlie wondered.

Robert was a few cells down the corridor and Kate was residing in the female block, separated from the male cells by the two interview rooms. It was not long before Charlie heard the jangle of keys.

"Here he comes," thought Charlie. "I wonder what they have in store for me now."

The heavy metal door creaked as it swung open.

"Hurry up, son," said the copper, a small, thin man with a mean face and large, protruding ears.

"This bloke reminds me of the F.A. Cup," thought Charlie. "It would be so tempting to grab his ears and try to lift him up."

"Come on lad, I haven't got all day, even if you have." snapped F.A. Cup.

"Sorry guv. I'm ready." Charlie scrambled to his feet and followed the jailer.

Charlie was taken to the sergeant's desk. He stood before the sergeant and waited for the lanky, bespectacled governor to speak.

"I feel like I am still at school waiting to see Father Freed for doing something naughty," mused the prisoner, "I remember praying that I wouldn't get caned. I was more scared then about forgetting my homework than I am now about all these burglaries."

"You shall be charged with three offences......" the sergeant read out.

Charlie tried to appear attentive. He gathered that he was to be charged with two burglaries and one theft. The other offences would be taken into consideration. This meant that the magistrates would know that he had committed them but he would not be formally charged.

The sergeant cleared his throat and informed that bail was to be opposed on the grounds that the likelihood of re-offending was substantial.

"Therefore," continued Lanky, "you shall be kept here overnight and will appear before the magistrates in the morning."

The stinking police cell awaited. F.A. Cup was only too pleased to escort Charlie to his accommodation.

"Where's Rob and Kate, guv?" asked Charlie before F.A. Cup slammed the door.

"Not here," sneered the officer, "they were both bailed some time ago."

"I bet he got bullied at school," thought Charlie. "He really seems to take pleasure in upsetting other people. Or, maybe his parents didn't show him any love while he was growing-up."

"I wonder why those two have been given bail and not me," thought Charlie, as he sat in his cell. "Probably because they helped the police when they were interviewed. I suppose the police look on me as the ringleader. At least they got that right."

Charlie paced the cell. He thought about his life and the avenues if followed.

"Everyone has a choice to do right or wrong." He recalled sitting in assembly listening to Father Freed.

"But have I had a choice," mused Charlie, "would I be in this state if I hadn't got these bloody thoughts?"

Charlie sat on the end of the wooden bench.

"Still, we had a laugh while it lasted" he consoled himself, "and if they lock me away in the morning at least I'll have got myself a cure. Hopefully my obsessions won't bother me when I get to prison."

He stretched-out on the thin mattress which nearly covered the bench.

"My life has definitely been dictated by my neurotic behaviour. I mean, at school I was enthusiastic and hard working; not to mention fairly intelligent. At my first school I was always at the top of the class or, at least very close to it. Now, here I am, preparing to go to jail. And that's without mentioning the other people I persuaded to join me with my crimes. I have to admit I manipulated all the others to start thieving."

Boredom crept up on Charlie.

"There's fuck all to do," he moaned, "how the hell am I gonna get used to this? I reckon the only thing is to have a sleep. At least I won't have to stare at these dirty walls for a few hours. I must have read the graffiti fifty times over."

He closed his eyes. Waves of resentment flooded his person.

"Why should I have to cope with all this shit just to feel normal?" he reasoned. "This room is dirty, smelly and soiled and the food is so fucking disgusting I wouldn't give it to my dog. My weird ideas have got me here, but surely it's not my fault if bloody thoughts keep forcing themselves into my head."

It was a distressed prisoner who finally fell into a fitful sleep.

The next morning, after a nauseating breakfast, Charlie's bail application beckoned.

"Must try and eat something," Charlie thought, "Might need my strength. Don't know what will happen today."

Charlie was handcuffed and driven to the magistrates' court. F.A. Cup was noted by his absence.

"Probably at home in bed," thought Charlie. "Might even be with some bird." He pictured F.A. Cup. "Well, maybe not."

The patrol car gained entry to the courtroom. Before Charlie was led from the car a massive gate closed to prevent any attempt at escape.

"No chance of doing a runner from here," mused Charlie.

Charlie was guided to some secure cells to await his hearing. John, the court's jailer, checked the young man was okay before closing the door.

"He seems nice," thought Charlie as, once again, he paced his cell.

After about seventy laps of the cell Charlie was visited by the duty solicitor. The learned gentleman appeared in a hurry. Charlie listened and agreed. It wouldn't matter what the solicitor said - Charlie couldn't care what happened. Charlie continued to pace the length of the cell.

"Bloody hell." he mumbled, "there has got to be more to life than this. I'm not sure how long I'll have to spend inside to cope with the bloody thoughts but I'm bored shitless already."

The door opened again.

"Brilliant," thought Charlie, "somebody to talk to. I don't care who it is, anyone will do."

Beside the bulky jailer stood a young, slightly built, studious looking chap.

"This is James. He is a key worker from a local bail hostel. He could be a great help to you," John said to Charlie.

"I didn't think he was the heavy mob come to whip my arse," Charlie thought to himself.

James sat with Charlie. The door remained slightly ajar.

"I believe we can help you," begun James. "If the magistrates are in agreement we could offer you accommodation as an alternative to prison. Your offences are not violent and they are not too serious for our hostel to be out of the question."

Charlie wasn't completely convinced.

"What about my bloody thoughts," wondered Charlie, "this bloke doesn't know about them. I wonder if he would be so keen to have me if he knew about them."

"I really do believe this is your best option." James' voice disturbed Charlie's thinking.

"Alright then," conceded Charlie, knowing when he was beaten.

James departed and the door was shut. Another fifty laps and the door opened.

"Come on mate," said John, "they're ready for you."

The prosecution briefly stated that the police were opposing bail on the grounds that there was a likelihood of the defendant committing further offences if given his liberty.

The duty solicitor, short and intelligent looking, arose. "My client h-h-has l-learnt an ex-ex-extremely h-harsh lesson by being arrested a-a-and w-w-would keep out o-of tr-tr-trouble to demonstrate h-his genuine re-remorse." he spluttered.

"I do not believe it," Charlie tried to conceal a grin, "he's only got a stammer. No wonder he didn't say much in the cells."

Charlie rubbed his nose.

"I bet he got bullied at school" his mind started to wander, "the little bastards probably hung him out of every window on the premises."

Charlie tried to force his attention on the matter in hand. He realized that Stutter was discussing the advantages of the bail hostel.

"I think i-it wo-wo-would be more b-b-beneficial than c-custody," he stammered.

"Hurry up, mate," Charlie thought, "before somebody dies. Those magistrates aren't as young as they used to be."

Eventually the duty solicitor concluded. The entire courtroom looked relieved. The magistrates retired to consider their options.

"They'll probably give me bail so they haven't got to listen to an appeal from Stutter," Charlie smiled to himself.

Charlie had to admit he was anxious.

"Don't worry," he told himself, "whatever they decide will be fine. If the hostel is no help to my thoughts I'll just have to rob something else."

It seemed like ages but was probably only a few minutes when the bell rang. Charlie knew what this meant - the magistrates had made a decision. Charlie's heart raced. His mouth was dry. He needed the toilet.

"We have decided to release you into the care of the bail hostel" the magistrate spoke softly but firmly, "however, rest assured, if your conditions set by the hostel are breached you will almost certainly find yourself in prison."

Charlie felt a slight sense of relief.

"My options are still open," he mused, "I can take a bit of time to think about what I am going to do now."

Charlie collected his few belongings from the cell.

"See ya, John," he said.

"Good luck," replied the jailer, "keep out of trouble."

"I'll try," replied Charlie, "but I'm making no promises."

The hostel was his future. For how long, he couldn't be certain.

"Okay," reflected Charlie, as he left the court building, "it's not jail but I don't reckon there'll be many old women in the hostel."

Chapter 6

The hostel, from the exterior, resembled a big, old country house.
"This looks quite posh," thought Charlie, "still I don't know what the other people will be like. A place can only be as good as the people who are in it."

He wandered into the vast hallway.

"Nothing to get in a state about, so far," decided Charlie.

The interior looked clean and cared for. Nothing flash, just pleasant.

"I hope that the other lads like me," mused Charlie, "first impressions are very important and I don't want everyone to think that I'm a right tosser. If I'm lucky I might find myself a few good mates. You never know when a good pal could come in handy."

Charlie soon found his room. A nice size, he was to share with two other residents. There were six other rooms; most of them housed three young men, the remainder a couple.

It wasn't long before Charlie met his two roommates. Carl, with his bright ginger hair and big mouth, soon made an impression.

"What a prick." decided Charlie, as he listened to Carl's tales of custody.

"The bloke has only done a couple of weeks," thought Charlie, "but the way he carries on you'd think that he had spent most of his life inside."

"Nobody fucked with me in Lewes," Carl droned on, "I didn't let nobody take the piss. When I had a fight I made sure that the other bloke got hurt."

"It doesn't take much brain to see what makes Carl tick" thought Charlie, as he lay on his bed staring at the wall, "he's obviously a complete loser and tries to impress people with his stories. Probably never had any mates all his life, just people who knocked the piss out of him. Now, he's trying to make sure that doesn't happen again by giving us all this shit."

The other lad in Charlie's room was completely different to Carl. Although he was twenty-three, he didn't physically appear old enough to have spent time in several adult jails. Jason was tall and thin with a very boyish face. He was sensible, quiet, respectful, even trustworthy.... in fact, everything that Carl wasn't.

"From what I've seen so far," thought Charlie, "I think I could trust Jason. He's not the type of bloke who would try and shag your bird. If you got into a fight he'd probably stand with you. On the other hand, there's Carl. Certainly not one to be trusted. He'd probably rob his own gran for the price of a pint."

Jason and Charlie spent hours chatting. When Carl wasn't around they put the world to rights. Jason told his mate how he had ended up in so many different prisons.

"Started thieving when I was quite young, eleven or twelve," he told Charlie, "as I got older the things that me and my mates did got more serious. Sooner or later the authorities get shagged of you and then prison is where you go. Once you've been inside, then nearly every time you go to court that is where you end up.

Charlie paid close attention. He liked to listen to other peoples' tales of woe. Then he could forget his own problems.

"Do ya reckon that you'll ever get sorted?" he asked Jason.

"Probation officers and people like that reckon if you do keep going back to prison then something has to change, on the outside, to stop you."

"Like what?" questioned Charlie.

"Well, if you meet a girl, fall in love, have a nipper... something along those lines," answered Jason.

Charlie soon adapted to his new surroundings and he really looked forward to his chats with Jason. The other lads in the hostel made the newcomer feel quite at ease so life wasn't unpleasant.

"Why did you start nicking, Charlie?" Jason asked during an evening natter.

"No particular reason" Charlie replied, "nothing better to do, easy money, I ain't really sure."

They talked a while longer until Jason decided he needed a bath.

"Don't want to turn into a smelly shit," he informed Charlie, as he left the room with his towel.

Carl was out with friends so Charlie had the room to himself.

"I like Jason" Charlie thought, "I even trust him but there ain't no way that I'm gonna tell him about those bloody thoughts. If he did take me seriously there is a good chance that he would turn against me. Then he would almost certainly tell the other lads and I'd be treated like a leper."

Charlie rolled over on his unmade bed.

"Good thing is," his mind continued to whirl, "the thoughts haven't bothered me since I've arrived at the hostel. I ain't sure why. Maybe it is because there are no old women about and I'm not likely to meet one. On the other hand, my days are so full with all the changes and the new people that there just ain't time for any distressing ideas to force their way into my mind."

The days passed, slowly at first, then much faster. Charlie and Jason spent much time walking by the nearby river. They chatted and enjoyed the rays from the sun while they tossed pebbles into the shimmering water.

One day, nearing the end of his first week, Charlie lazed on his bed gazing out of the window. His mind wandered.

"What next," he pondered, "will this be the cure? A short spell in here and I'll be okay. Is it too late to get back on track....?"

"Charlie." Jason's voice broke Charlie's deliberations, "do ya fancy a trip down town?"

"Eh yeah, okay then" Charlie replied.

"Great. Spud wants to come with us; is that okay with you?"

"No problem" answered Charlie.

The trio wandered through the town, laughing and joking. Spud had this habit of making rude comments about passers-by. Charlie worried a shopping trip could end in a visit to casualty. They passed a young woman walking her dog.

"Why take your dog to the shops," Spud voiced his concerns, "still, if I'm honest, I'd rather shag the thing on the end of the lead."

An old woman shuffled past.

"On her way to her own funeral" laughed Spud.

"Did I hit her?" The thought was inside Charlie's head. He didn't have a clue where it came from and he certainly hadn't seen it creeping-up.

"Well, that arrived with a bang" panicked Charlie, as he turned to check the welfare of the elderly lady.

He stared intently after his subject. Apart from a limp, of which Charlie had been previously aware, she seemed fine. Charlie stared a little longer than was necessary, just to be sure. He knew only too well that he wasn't the easiest person to convince. Satisfied, he turned back towards his mates. He felt something lightly brush against his arm. He glanced at the offending article. A shopping bag - held by a pensioner... a female pensioner.

"Oh hell." he cursed. "Did I hurt her?"

"Don't be so bloody stupid," he told himself. "She's carried on walking. If you'd have hurt her she'd have fallen on the floor."

He decided quickly.

"Jay, Spud... I've just spotted an old mate from school. I'm gonna have a chat."

Without waiting for a reply he hurried after the old lady. He just had to be certain that she was unharmed. By now, Charlie had realised that the obtrusive thoughts were here to stay. He felt the familiar anxiety build-up, uncontrolled, inside him. His heartbeat thudded, fast and furious. His lips became numb and his extremities shook. His mouth desired any form of lubrication and his eyes were, for the duration, certainly not going to focus.

"Got to get back to the hostel" Charlie tried to think clearly, "then I can try and calm myself."

He made it. He couldn't be sure how but he found his way home. He grabbed a paper bag from the bin and breathed deeply into it. As he regained control of his breathing he started to feel a lot more relaxed.

"Thank the Lord for that," thought Charlie, "but I should imagine a lot worse is to come. Now the thoughts have started to bother me while I am here.... well, I don't know what I should do."

Charlie felt quite low. He lay on his unmade bed and pondered.

"There is only one answer," he decided, "I'll have to go back to plan A - prison. Then, there is no chance of meeting an old woman. I doubt I'll have to go down to a shopping centre if I'm serving in one of Her Majesty's establishments."

Charlie felt a little better. He had made a definite decision. He needed to finalise the details but he was sure that he had booked himself a one-way ticket to the prison gates.

The days, as you might expect, continued to roll along. The intrusive thoughts bothered Charlie, sometimes greatly, but he could see an end. Prison was, for this disturbed young man, the only lifeline.

A few days later in the week Charlie wandered into the kitchen. As expected, he found Tony and Duncan, a couple of his closest pals.

"Time to test the water," he thought, glancing at each young man's cuisine.

"I wouldn't eat that shit," he decided, looking at the slop on Tony's plate, "it looks like it's already been through somebody's system."

Duncan's dinner looked quite tempting.

"Yep, that's okay," thought Charlie, "and I never imagined Dunc as a cook."

"Alright," began Charlie, "I guessed that I'd find you here."

"Not much else to do" answered Tony, tall and slim.

Depending on how Tony dressed often made his build seem very different. Sometimes he would appear athletic; wouldn't look out of place on a soccer field. Nevertheless, on occasions, he could look so thin a gust of wind would whip him away. Charlie had liked Tony from day one. He admired his confidence, yet never felt his pal to be arrogant.

"Where you been today?" interrupted Duncan, not wanting to be ignored any longer.

Duncan, fairly short and rotund, liked to be the centre of attention. He certainly wasn't going to allow Charlie and Tony to have a gossip without being included.

"Oh, nowhere special" Charlie replied, "just sitting about pondering my future."

"Sounds interesting" laughed Duncan, "so what you gonna do? You could always rob Barclays or shag some rich tart."

"This should be a doodle," thought Charlie, "I'm definitely in the best place to find people to thieve with. Most of them don't know any other way to get money."

"Well" began Charlie, "this life ain't for me. I mean what type of life have they given us? We've got fuck all. So I reckon I'll do some nicking and see what happens. If I get caught then, yeah, I will go to prison but so what? As they've given me nothing what have I got to lose? At least, when I get out my life is my own. If I get away with it, then great. A bit of extra money; the odd luxury... things must improve."

Tony didn't need asking twice. The oldest of the three residents had done years behind bars and found that way of life the easiest.

"I'm with you, mate," he said, "I agree this place is a shit-hole and I don't reckon that we've anything to lose."

"That was bloody easy," reasoned Charlie, "at least I won't have to wander about, on my own, worrying that I've battered some old biddy."

Duncan wasn't quite so eager. He had been to prison once previously and didn't want to repeat the experience.

"Oh, come on Dunc," urged Tony, "we'll have a good laugh and probably won't get nicked."

"You've got to admit," added Charlie, "this place is a hole."

"Alright," Duncan agreed reluctantly.

"Peer pressure," decided Charlie, "brilliant."

That night, around twelve, the three residents gathered in the hostel's entrance.

"You both okay?" whispered Tony.

The others nodded. Making as little sound as possible the group made a hasty exit.

"So, anyone got a plan?" questioned Tony.

"Let's just get away from here," answered Duncan, "we don't want to get nicked before we've done anything."

They padded silently along, heading towards the town centre.

"I reckon," offered Duncan, "chore a motor and then drive around looking for something to take."

"Sounds favourite," agreed Charlie.

The trio trudged onwards.

"There might be something down here," whispered Tony, indicating a dimly lit side road, "let's have a quick butchers."

The road was gloomy mimicking their mood. Nonetheless, the three cheered considerably when an unoccupied vehicle was spotted.

"What do ya reckon, Tubbs? You're the car thief," asked Tony. "You have got that screwdriver, ain't you?"

"Course I have," answered Duncan.

"Well, what about it?" pressed Tony.

"Why not?" came the reply. Quickly and quietly Duncan forced open the driver's door.

"Here we go," thought Charlie, "no turning back, now."

Duncan was busily trying to force the steering lock. This manoeuvre proved much more difficult than anticipated. Duncan grunted and groaned.

"It's all that bloody flab," jeered Tony, "are you getting there, Tubbs?"

"I've never had one this stiff before," grunted Duncan.

"Keep trying, mate," encouraged Charlie.

The screeching alarm started without warning. The three lads looked at each other; no reaction... yet.

"Fuck me," cursed Charlie, "what the hell have you done, Dunc?"

"Fuck knows," gasped Duncan, as he struggled from the car, "let's just get out of here."

"You shit," cursed Tony, "you said it would be a piece of piss. Come on, let's fuck-off."

They did. For ten minutes they wheezed and panted away from the damaged vehicle.

"No police," gasped Tony, "we should be alright."

"I can't understand what went wrong," exclaimed Duncan, "shall we try again?"

The trio wandered along road after road looking for a vehicle to steal.

"Maybe this is a sign" thought Charlie, as he plodded along.

"Don't be such a prick," he told himself, "the only reason we ain't got a motor is because Duncan is a liar. The prat said he could nick any car..... well, now we know, he bloody can't."

An angry Tony, a disappointed Charlie and a puffing Duncan trudged many different roads and some the same.

"Look, we ain't gonna get a car tonight," moaned Tony to the others, "our best plan is to go back to the hostel and hope we ain't been missed. I just need some kip. We'll try again tomorrow."

It was almost four o'clock when the trio arrived at the hostel..... completely exhausted. Charlie collapsed onto his bed He just lay still waiting for sleep to come to his rescue. He couldn't even be bothered to remove his dungarees.

"What the hell is happening to me," he thought as he drifted into a slumber, "I steal because of the bloody thoughts... I don't get anything... don't even get nicked... hell, what can I do...? Will the thoughts go if I'm sent to prison? Will they be here when I get out...."

Eventually sleep ended the torment.... temporarily.

The following morning dawned lovely and sunny. Not so for Charlie, Tony and Duncan. They had to go and see Mr. White, the main man, in the hostel's office.

"It has been noted that the three of you breached your curfews," began Mr. White, "I don't want any excuses and I have to tell you that this is your first and final warning. You may leave."

That afternoon Duncan, Tony and Charlie were seated in Tony's room; as thick as thieves.

"You two stay here," said Duncan, "I've been doing a bit of thinking and I've had a bit of an idea."

"Oh yeah," moaned Tony, "what are you going to do? Learn how to nick a car?"

"I'm gonna use the phone," answered Duncan, "give me a minute."

"I'd like to give you something," mumbled Tony, as Duncan left the group, "and it ain't a fucking minute."

Fifteen minutes and Duncan returned with a big grin covering his podgy face.

"I've spoke to a pal of mine," he explained, "and he's told me about a council depot where the keys are left in the trucks. Once you're in the depot any shit could manage it."

"Even you?" mocked Tony.

Duncan didn't rise to the bait.

"Duncan wouldn't be stupid enough to argue with Tony," thought Charlie, "he's scared of him. I like Tony but I wouldn't want him for an enemy, either."

After a day of waiting the trio were more than ready for that night.

"Once I leave here tonight," thought Charlie, "that's it... no going back. The thoughts will have driven me to prison. Will that be the end of it? I don't know. I hope so.... but, somehow, I doubt it."

The rusty gate swung open. No resistance.

"Sweet," whispered Tony, "that was bloody quick."

"I could pull a bird quicker," sniggered Duncan.

"The only thing you'll be pulling is your plonker if we get nicked so, for fuck's sake, hurry up." snapped Tony.

"I can't imagine Tubbs with some piece," mused Charlie, letting his mind wander from the task in hand, "I mean, what young lovely would want some old hippo on top of her?"

Charlie snapped back into reality. Everything was as expected. The trucks were ready for the taking. A dream for any car thief who couldn't steal a car. The three escapees had a rough plan.

"One of these should go through a jeweller's window, including the metal shutter," said Charlie.

"Hopefully," commented Tony. "We can but try."

The trip began with Duncan erratically driving the truck. The driver chatted.... rubbish, complete and utter undiluted crap.

"There was this one sort mad for it," he drivelled, "she was tall but curvaceous with it. Mind you, I've never had a problem with skinny birds. One night I met a lovely blonde tart. I took her outside the club and found a nice quiet alley. I swear, she squirmed in my arms."

"Probably trying to get away," interrupted Charlie.

"Piss off, wanker," responded Duncan.

"I wonder if he's trying to convince me and Tony or himself" thought Charlie, "it's obvious to anyone with half a brain that all these models wouldn't go for Tubbs."

Charlie glanced at Tony.

"He might be going to a swingers' party," thought Charlie, "he looks so calm. I'm supposed to need to go to prison, yet I'm shitting myself. Still, I suppose he's spent nearly ten years inside why worry about a few more? As for me, I've only heard what it's like inside, never actually done it."

"Are we nearly there, Dunc" asked Tony, interrupting Charlie's deliberations.

"Yeah, I reckon so, mate," replied the driver.

They drove past the jeweller's shop.

"Let's park for a minute before we do it," said Tony.

"Good idea," agreed Charlie, desperately trying to stay in control.

"Okay, I saw a place," answered Duncan.

The truck came to rest on a common near the shop.

"I just hope that I'm doing the best thing" panicked Charlie, suffering last minute nerves.

"You okay, Chaz" asked Duncan, resting his chin on the steering wheel.

"Yeah, no problem" mumbled Charlie, "but I could do with a smoke."

"I don't reckon these two would think a lot of me if they knew my real motives," decided Charlie.

Duncan handed Charlie and Tony a roll-up and soon the inside of the truck resembled a sauna.

"Five years," thought Charlie, trying to appear calm, "God knows if I'll manage."

The smoke hung in the air.

"Do ya reckon this'll be a nice little earner?" Duncan asked his two passengers.

"It shouldn't be too bad," answered Charlie, "just pray the police don't get there. We wouldn't have a prayer if we were chased."

"This ain't the quickest, is it?" asked Duncan.

It came from somewhere and it came rather fast. A brilliant light blinded Charlie.

"What the hell's happening...." he mumbled.

There was no reply but the strain etched on the faces of Tony and Duncan said more than enough.

"Trouble," panicked Charlie, "and lots of it."

The door was roughly pulled open and a torch pointed inside

"Police - don't move." the voice was loud and deep.

"This is it," thought Charlie, "the beginning of the end of suffering the thoughts or will it just be the start of something worse?"

As Tony and Duncan were dragged from the truck Charlie's thoughts were of all the little old ladies he'd never harmed.

"I never would hurt somebody so defenceless so is this really the only way?" he asked himself.

The answer was a yanking on his jacket. It was time to leave the truck.

"We've a right bunch of poofters here, guv." jeered a flashy, young constable, as he pulled a packet of condoms from Duncan's pocket.

"I often get lucky," mumbled Duncan, "and classy women like a bloke to be prepared."

"What classy bird would look at a fat loser like you?" sneered the flashy detective.

"What a wanker," thought Charlie, "and who would look at an arrogant tosser like him."

Charlie did have to admit that the condoms were unopened. He would also have to admit that he wasn't the least bit surprised. Poor Duncan.... he did like to dream.

The handcuffs were snapped on Charlie's wrists. Then the constable firmly guided him to a separate car from his pals and the journey to the local station began.

"Might as well get used to this crap," decided Charlie, "if this is what it takes to manage my thoughts then I should even try to enjoy it."

Charlie hadn't been in the police station for very long when he was brought before the custody sergeant. He was charged, as he had expected, with the unlawful taking of a motor vehicle and refused bail.

"You'll appear before the Magistrate in the morning," the sergeant told him.

That lonely night as Charlie lay in his filthy cell he desperately tried to remain positive.

"You've got to look on the bright side," he told himself, "at least they nicked you before you got to the jeweller's. If you'd have done that job you'd be looking at five years. Now, you'll probably only get a few months; a year at the worst. So you'll know if prison is the answer to the bloody thoughts. If it is, then you can always get put back inside. That certainly won't be too difficult."

Charlie covered himself with the tatty blanket. He thought about his schooldays, his parents, his sister and much more but not old women. So far, so good.

The sun shone brightly the following morning.

"What a cracking day," thought Charlie, as he gazed out the cell's tiny window, "still I certainly won't be sitting by a river with some lovely. To be honest, even if I was a free man, my best hope would be some old porker with a spotty face."

The three prisoners arrived at the court. They were all refused bail. They were returned to the cells under the court to wait for the prison van. Duncan and Charlie, both being under twenty-one, would be taken to Feltham Young Offenders' Institution. It was here that they would wait to be sentenced. The likelihood of bail being granted before sentence was slim. Tony, an adult by law, would be remanded to Wormwood Scrubs Prison. Tony wasn't fazed in the slightest.

"Four fucking walls are four fucking walls," said Tony to Charlie, "wherever they are."

"I suppose so," replied Charlie, desperately wishing that he felt as calm as Tony looked.

They chatted for a while but, finally, silence fell.

"Right," Charlie told himself, "I've done it. I've had the guts to get here. Now, hopefully, I won't have any problems from inside my warped head."

He did realise that the unwanted thoughts had vanished. Certainly not without trace... but, for now, they were gone.

"I know why," Charlie decided, "my mind is filled with so much, I haven't got any room for thoughts of old women. At the moment I'm more worried about prison - are all the rumours true? Will I survive? Will anything horrible happen to me? What the bloody hell will the next few months be like?"

The cell door opened.

"Let's go lads," said the jailer.

"We all choose a path to follow," thought Charlie, "but did I choose this one or was it forced upon me? Whichever it was, I must play the part. I can survive this and I fucking will."

Charlie tried to stop shaking as he headed for the van.

Chapter 7

"Are we nearly there?" Charlie enquired, glancing at the lad who had the dubious pleasure of sharing a pair of handcuffs.

"Not far mate," replied Richard, a skinny youth with greasy hair who, obviously, had a severe acne problem.

"Have you been here before?" asked Charlie, desperate to gather as much information as he could about the infamous place.

"No I ain't," said Richard, "but my aunt and uncle live near the prison."

"Are you on remand?" Charlie asked, knowing that remand and convicted prisoners were held at Feltham.

"No, convicted," replied the spotty youth, "I got five days because I didn't pay a fine."

"Bloody hell" thought Charlie, "is it worth all this effort for less than a week?"

It didn't seem long until before the vehicle stopped at some huge, heavy, metal gates.

"Here we go," thought Charlie, "could this be the cure to all my problems?"

The van entered the jail, a modern building surrounded by beautifully tended gardens.

"This doesn't look all that bad," decided Charlie, "apart from the fences it could be a holiday resort. It's hard to imagine all the horrible things going on when you see the place from the outside. Still that bloke my mum knows had a rough time in this very place. He was beaten-up daily; once, so bad that he nearly died. It was only the quick thinking of an officer that stopped him leaving this place in a wooden box."

It wasn't long before Charlie was seated in the jail's reception. A large cage with a wooden bench around the perimeter. The twenty or thirty young men in this cage made little, if any, noise.

"This lot look well pissed-off," thought Charlie, "some seem to be angry whereas many of 'em look like they are shitting themselves. I suppose they've heard rumours about jail and ain't too keen to find out if there is any truth in them. Blokes who have been here before are probably pissed-off that they're here again."

Charlie glanced briefly at a young black lad. The poor bastard, only about seventeen, looked closed to tears.

"I wonder why he did the crime," reflected Charlie, "he must have known there was a chance he could end-up inside. Still, who knows, look why I've ended-up in here."

Charlie looked at the bloke directly opposite. The scar from his eye to his chin made up most of his face.

"I wonder how he got that," thought Charlie, "probably best not to ask."

Charlie quickly glanced round the room.

"Still," he thought, I'd rather get a few slaps than have to worry about these fucking thoughts. I mean the thoughts nearly caused me to hang myself from the nearest lamp-post - the worst this place can do is finish me off."

Every twenty-five minutes or so, a group of names were called. Soon, as expected, an officer opened the cage.

"Hughes, Hamilton, Goodman, Lloyd and Kaunda. Follow me."

The lads stripped in the reception area and gave their clothes to an officer on duty. Then came an icy shower.

"Bloody hell" thought Charlie, "I could think of many better ways to spend my time."

"With the thoughts," he answered himself, "there ain't a lot else you could be doing. Have you seen any old women in here?"

When the officer decided, the group were allowed to step from the blasts of the shower and dress. Prison uniform for unconvicted inmates was brown jeans and a blue and white stripy shirt.

"These clothes are shit," thought Charlie, "still, I definitely don't want to be fancied in here so who cares what I look like. I won't be going to any discos for a while."

Charlie was escorted to another holding cell, identical to the first, and told to wait.

When all the newcomers had been processed officers from different wings started to arrive to take their new charges to their cells.

"It must be my turn soon" thought Charlie, "this is worse than waiting to have a tooth out."

"Barnes, Ihonor, Lloyd and Martin" ordered the balding, overweight, red-faced warden.

"Fat bastard," thought Charlie. "He looks a sadistic fucker."

"You lot will all be on my unit - Quail" he grunted.

"All the units are named after birds," reflected Charlie.

"Come-on, hurry-up." snapped the warden.

"I wonder if he's married," considered Charlie, as he followed the others, "surely no woman deserves that."

As Charlie neared the unit he felt anxious, to say the least.

"I've got to admit I am shitting it," Charlie panicked, "this is nearly as bad as the thoughts."

Charlie felt that he had left his stomach in reception. He struggled to walk in a straight line.

"Is it these bloody shoes they've given me or have my legs turned to jelly?"

Two black inmates just in front of Charlie discussed one of their pals on Quail. This lad had, supposedly, had a fight with a policeman and stabbed him with a screwdriver.

Very soon the longest walk of Charlie's life came to an end. The group reached a barred gate. Through the closely spaced steel, the inmates of Quail unit were on view. Playing pool, watching television, laughing and joking or just lazing about.

"Blimey," panicked Charlie, "this looks fucking terrible. Some of those blokes could eat me alive and shit out the pieces. Some of those black guys are well over six foot and at least seventeen stones."

The noise was deafening. Not disco deafening - deafening by intimidation.

The new inmates were shown to the wing probation office. They had a brief chat with a woman who had obviously never been to prison.

"If any other inmate picks on you tell an officer," prattled Mrs Hunt, "don't suffer in silence."

"Crap," thought Charlie, "do that and you're in the hospital. The only rule is that there ain't no rules and the officers don't have any say in what happens in here. I know that and I ain't even got to my cell."

After Mrs Hunt had chatted rubbish for a few minutes the newcomers were each escorted to their cells. Most cells were single but there were a few catering for two or four young men. Charlie was escorted to a single cell. The warden said nothing as he slammed the metal door.

"Keep calm" Charlie encouraged himself, "you knew this would happen sooner or later. What choice did you have? I'm just pleased that you've had the nerve to come this far, at least you are trying to deal with your problem."

Charlie wandered to the barred window. The view was lovely - another unit the same as his. He could see into the cells and, if he wanted, watch the other inmates. He glanced from one cell to another.

"What you staring at, wanker?" The voice was loud and threatening.

Charlie was stunned into silence. He assumed that an inmate on the other unit was yelling at him. He failed to utter a sound.

"Fuck yourself." The response came from a cell on Charlie's unit. The cell must have been quite close to his. "Do you want to sort it?"

"No mate," replied the inmate from the other unit. No aggression in his tone, this time.

"Well fuck yourself, star, you pussy."

"I wonder who that was," thought Charlie, "he must have a bit of respect."

Charlie paced the cell. He still didn't know what to expect. He thought back to when he was given his 'common entrance' exam results. He remembered pacing the school corridors waiting for the teacher to tell him if he made the grades - did he feel worse then than he did now?

A knocking on the wall startled Charlie.

"Next door, are you there?"

"What's up?" Charlie replied, feeling a little uneasy.

"You ain't got a skin, have you mate?" The voice was relaxed, perhaps even friendly.

"A what?" queried Charlie.

"A Rizla."

69

"Yeah," answered Charlie, "what do you want me to do with it?"

"You ain't been inside before, have you?" asked the voice.

"First time," Charlie answered.

"Well then," replied the mystery voice, "I'm Grant and this is your lucky day. For two ciggies I'll tell you all the rules you need to know while you are in here. I should know as I've been in one place or another for at least eight years. This time they'll probably give me an eight - the bastards do not like aggravated burglary."

"Ciggies?" queried Charlie.

"Proper smokes. Not roll-ups but a proper cigarette."

Grant and Charlie talked for most of the night.

"Association," said Grant, "that can be a bit dodgy. It's only a couple of hours a day but there is enough trouble. There's always some shit trying to tax somebody else."

"What do you mean by tax?"

"They try and take your fags or your candy," answered Grant, but just tell 'em to fuck 'emselves or the dirty slags will be back all the fucking time."

The next day. First association. Charlie kept himself to himself. Spoke briefly to Grant but, mainly, sat alone. Suddenly tribes of wardens rushed to the pool room. One inmate was carried from the room; another dragged.

"What happened?" Charlie asked Grant.

"Some nutter stabbed another bloke in the eye with a pencil."

First association - first drama.

At night the prison came to life. Charlie could hear at least ten conversations from his window.

"I'll kill you in the morning, you shit."

"You're mother gives good head."

"What you in for?"

"Burglary."

"Buggery, more like, you fucking nonce."

Others just sang. That was even worse.

The days blended and Charlie started to relax. He wasn't particularly happy but he did seem to be coping. He would admit that he was tenser before an association than after but he no longer dreaded leaving the security of his cell.

Charlie had nearly done a week. It was association and Charlie was sitting in his cell putting the finishing touches on a letter to his sister. Enter - three powerfully built black inmates. They pushed the door to avoid any unwanted attention.

"Oh hell" panicked Charlie, "here we go. I wonder what the hospital wing is like."

He studied his surroundings. Nowhere to run.

"What the bloody hell should I do? If I start to scream every shit on the unit will think I'm a wanker."

"Give us your snout," snarled one of the gang.

Charlie looked at the tall, athletically built man complete with shaven head and struggled with the urge to give-up smoking.

"If you give-in to the fuckers they'll keep coming back," Grant had always maintained.

"I've found a cure for my problems on the street," thought Charlie, "and I ain't gonna let three shits take it away from me."

Easier said than done.

"Come on" Charlie urged himself, "whatever they do to you can't be as bad as those thoughts."

"If you want it then come and fucking take it."

The three black youths looked shocked. Charlie looked terrified. He knew the damage was done; he could hardly laugh, hand-over the tobacco and tell them he had been joking.

"You're fucking dead." growled the same spokesman. He spat the words to add venom to their meaning.

He needn't have bothered - Charlie had already nearly pissed himself.

His hip whipped forward as his muscled arm shot-out. Charlie's nose cracked. Blood spurted. Charlie staggered backwards.

"If you hit the deck, you'll get hurt - bad." Grant had always said.

Charlie had believed him - he had no desire to test the statement.

"Slag" snorted the black youth, throwing a sharp left hook.

Charlie anticipated the punch and moved his head in the same direction. This would minimise contact - damage limitation.

"Hurt at least one of them." Charlie could hear Grant's words of wisdom rebounding in his brain, as his brain rebounded against his skull.

"I ain't come here to be used as a punch-bag" Charlie thought, lashing-out with as much force as he could manage.

The blow connected. More blood. Not a lot - but a visible amount. The black inmate's mouth showed signs of a struggle.

"Thank Christ for that," thought Charlie, "at least he knows he's had a bit of a bundle."

Enter the other two prisoners. Obviously unable to resist the temptation of a bloody brawl. Charlie felt the force of the first few blows before he fell to the ground. The kicks rained hard into his torso. His frame jolted but he'd passed the pain barrier. He grunted and groaned but was totally unable to shout. Seconds later the thrashing ended. Little, if anything, was said as the gang ambled from the cell.

Charlie lay, motionless, on the cell floor.

"Bastards… bastards…" he groaned, "they nearly fucking killed me.

Looking at all this blood I'm lucky to be breathing. I hope that the shits ain't done any permanent damage."

Charlie looked, from a swollen and bleeding eye, at the wooden table next to his bed. His tobacco had gone.

"Shit," he groaned, "I've taken all that battering and I still ain't gonna have a smoke tonight."

He very carefully manoeuvred himself onto the prison bed.

"Slowly," he mumbled to himself, "don't make matters any worse than they are already."

He lay still, breathing heavily.

"I could really do with a nice nurse, right now," he thought, "or any young lady. I just need a bit of care and attention."

He was aware that his injuries were still bleeding.

"Don't be such a ponce," he told himself, "you'll be okay. Just get a grip and stop feeling sorry for yourself. If you did have a young lovely in here for an hour or so you certainly wouldn't waste any time putting on a plaster."

He gazed at the writing on the ceiling.

"Is prison really so wonderful" he thought.

"What options have you got with your mental state," he answered himself, "at least, in here, you're normal. Every fucker gets beaten-up in this place."

He tested each extremity in turn. Everything seemed to be in working order. The rest of association he lay in bed.... in pain.

The warden checked the cell and slammed the door. Association was over.

"I've certainly had better days," groaned Charlie, as he decided it was far too painful to roll over in his bed.

As the days passed, Charlie's injuries improved. He didn't look forward to associations but he had made a few pals.

One association, Charlie and Michael, a mate on the unit, stood by the television having a chat.

"Have you had a shower on this unit, yet?" asked Michael.

"No, not yet," answered Charlie, "I wash in the cell every night but I will jump under the shower very soon. Why do you ask? Do I smell or something?"

"No" answered Michael, "I haven't had a shower since I've been in Feltham. I strip every night in the cell and wash all-over."

"Why?" asked Charlie.

"Well the showers are a risky place. It just ain't worth the risk. They'll give you a beating in there just to show you who's the boss. If some shit has had a bad day, got a bit of bad news from the outside, he might wait in the shower for the first unlucky sod who goes in there. I prefer to wash in my cell and keep out of trouble, if I can."

Charlie looked at Michael, stockily built, average height, four inch scar on his right cheek and shaven head and wondered if he should take his pal's advice.

"It probably is the most sensible thing to do," he thought to himself, "but I need to feel normal. I'm probably gonna have to spend many years in places like this so I can't start being scared. If I was only gonna be here for a few weeks I wouldn't bother with the showers but with my mind I can see many long years behind bars."

"Right lads, behind your doors. Association is over."

"Later Charlie," said Michael as he turned towards his cell.

"See you at breakfast, Mickey," answered Charlie.

Charlie read for a while, had a wash, cleaned his teeth and, then, climbed into bed. Before sleep rescued him from Feltham he had decided tomorrow he would take a nice, hot shower.

"You mustn't be intimidated" he persuaded himself, "you've as much right to a shower as anyone. Remember what Grant said."

His dreams took him far away from Feltham's infamous institution.

The next day, after two inedible meals, Charlie's door swung open for association. He picked-up his white towel and prison-issue soap.

"Now or never," he decided, "if I lose my bottle now I'll never have a proper wash."

He strolled towards the washroom.

"I ain't scared" he lied to himself, "I ain't gonna let these bastards stop me from having a shower."

He plodded into the shower-block….. empty.

"Thank fuck for that," he mumbled, desperately trying to relax, "this lot in here are obviously dirty bastards."

Charlie chose a cubicle and undressed quickly. He wanted to leave this part of the prison as soon as he possibly could.

"If you're gonna shit yourself the whole time that you are in here, then is there any point?" he asked himself.

He gasped as the icy water splashed against his pale body. Owing to several trips to the prison gym and a lack of tasty food his shape had improved.

"I'm almost anaemic," he decided. "I certainly need to get some sun."

He started to enjoy the feel of the water as it became warmer.

"I would love to laze about on a beach," he decided.

"With the thoughts entering your head?" the question had to be asked.

"I suppose I would struggle," he admitted.

"I'll just have to turn the light off when I'm with a lovely," he decided, casting another disapproving look at his lily-white frame.

Charlie lifted his face so the water would wash-away his problems. A few seconds he could forget where he was. He could forget the beatings he had witnessed and received, the crap he had been given to eat and the degrading treatment handed-out. He could be anywhere he wanted with whoever he wanted. Just for a few seconds.

"That's better," he thought, as he finished washing, "no problem."

The calm before the storm.

"You're in my shower. Piss off." The deafening voice, to say the least, made Charlie jump.

"Don't worry," he encouraged himself, "it's probably some prat trying to act like a man."

He stepped from the shower and wrapped his towel around his waist.

"Ain't got much to hide but I feel really awkward naked in front of some geezer having a pop."

Charlie struggled to maintain a grip of his nerves. He knew better than to show fear even if that is exactly what he felt.

"Must be a nutter," Charlie decided, "or some shit who's had a letter from his girlfriend saying that she's going with his best mate. Whatever the score can't let him take the piss."

Charlie wasn't overly keen to fight but he realised that he would have few other options.

"Don't want any of this crap" he thought, "but as I've got no choice got to try and go in hard. Don't want this fucking loon to get the smell of blood."

Charlie took a step towards the tall, slim, black male.

"It ain't got your name on it - so fuck off." he tried to sound threatening.

The lanky inmate suddenly lunged and grabbed Charlie. This took Charlie by surprise - he had been expecting a punch. They struggled, both trying to gain an advantage. Trying to find an opening to deliver a telling blow. Like a game of squash - you play the point waiting for a chance to hit a winner. Charlie's towel fell to the ground. He had been trying to prevent this from happening but, in the end, it had been a straight choice between several punches to his head or taking his hand from the towel.

"You're dead man" snarled the black youth, "I'm gonna blast you up."

The black prisoner was first to free an arm. Charlie felt a sharp pain in his eye. The taller man had cut Charlie's eye with, what appeared to be, a very sharp thumb-nail.

"Fucker," moaned Charlie, desperately trying to roll on top of the other youth.

The surprising power of the black inmate kept Charlie pinned to the washroom floor.

"Got to keep trying" panicked Charlie, "don't know when this shit will leave it."

The taller man pushed Charlie's bald head, again and again, against the stone floor.

Each thud frightened Charlie, more and more.

"How far is he going to go" he tried to think clearly, but found it increasingly difficult with each thud becoming louder.

Charlie pulled his right arm from under the black youth's leg, which had kept it pinned to the ground. Now or never. He had little strength remaining. He had to take this chance. He lashed at the black inmate's face. His clenched hand connected forcibly. It's amazing the strength that can be gained from fear. Charlie pulled back his hand and struck again. The taller youth stopped using Charlie's head to flatten the washroom floor. Charlie hit him again. Blood was clearly visible on his face. The black man stood up.

"Dead man" he muttered and left. That was it. Gone but certainly not forgotten.

"All that bloody fuss and he didn't even use the shower," Charlie muttered as he struggled to his feet at the second attempt.

His head was pounding and traces of blood dripped from his left eye but, being a clever chap, he knew that events could have been much nastier.

A few days later and Charlie's door opened for association. He strolled over to Gary, a friend who had been on the unit for a couple of days. Gary, a short, slimly-built lad with a clear complexion and neatly combed brown hair certainly didn't look the type.

"I could imagine him helping his Nan with the shopping or baby-sitting his little sister," mused Charlie, "not robbing a shop or mugging some bloke."

Gary was on remand for fraud. He had been in Feltham a few weeks and hated every second. On a different unit he had been so badly bullied that he had drunk a bottle of shampoo to get himself transferred to the hospital. He had been sent to the hospital and, then, found himself on the same unit as Charlie.

"Why did you break the law?" asked Charlie, "you don't seem like most of them in here."

"Well" answered Gary, "you remember I told you about my girlfriend, Tania? Anyway her sister was seriously ill in Holland and Tania wanted to visit. She needed money. I'd do anything for her and, well, here I am."

"Fraud ain't that serious," said Charlie, "can't you get a bit of bail?"

Three black troublemakers strolled towards Gary and Charlie.

"Want your tobacco this week, Gary, my soldier," snorted the first of the three, "if you don't deliver you'll be back in the hospital. Understand?"

The trio sauntered away obviously looking for more victims.

"Lots of bastards in here," Charlie stated the obvious, his voice kept low, "what about bail, Gary, any chance?"

"Well, I'm in court on Monday and my solicitor reckons that I've a chance."

After bang-up on Sunday evening Charlie lay in his cell wondering what his friends were doing back home. His thoughts turned to Gary.

"I wonder if he'll get bail tomorrow" he thought, "it would be great for him if he did but he is my best mate on this unit so who will I talk to?"

"Don't be so selfish," he told himself, "course I hope he gets out. He's already got blokes on his case and I'll get to know other people."

"It's weird, ain't it?" Charlie mused, "You want your mate to get out because it's best for him but, on the other hand, you're left on your own."

Gary went to court on the Monday. Charlie never saw him again.

"Well" decided Charlie, "either he got bail or the screws have transferred him to a different unit. I really hope that he got out because, I reckon, he'll get shit wherever they put him."

One day was much the same as the next.

"This must be what it's like to go to work in a job you hate," thought Charlie, lying on an identical bed in an identical cell.

The routine was broken each week with a trip to court - further remand. Back to Feltham. Maybe a new unit, maybe not. Every unit looked the same and the personnel differed only in name. You always seemed to get your bullies, your nutters, your 'copers' and your bullied. Friends, on each unit, came and went. Some turned into true pals, others befriended then used you. The good mates you remembered - there were fewer of them. The food was awful but consistent. It must be possible to build a tolerance, Charlie had decided.

Raven unit was the next setting for Charlie. He had been allocated here after his last remand.

"Wonder what this'll be like," thought Charlie, as he lay in his single cell waiting for his first association, "hope there ain't too many troublemakers."

"The new bloke is a nonce," yelled the unknown voice.

"What the bloody-hell did he say that for?" panicked Charlie. "Is he talking about me?"

"He's probably sitting in his cell waiting for his name," the voice continued.

"Blimey," thought Charlie, "wonder what's going on here. Either they've got the wrong bloke or they're winding me up. If they're trying to get me worried they've done a good job. I just hope that I don't go out for association and get flattened. I'll just have to keep calm and wait and see what happens."

Association came unaccompanied by trouble. Charlie spoke to a chap called Mark. The pair seemed to find a common ground for discussion.

"What's this unit like then?" asked Charlie.

"Not a lot different from the others," answered Mark, "there is quite a bit of trouble.

You see the black geezer by the television - big bloke - well, he is always kicking off. He might try and have your tobacco, so be careful."

As Mark spoke a small, slightly built white inmate walked towards the black male and handed him some tobacco. They certainly weren't mates so it was obvious what was happening.

"I see what you mean," replied Charlie, "I'll certainly be watching-out for him."

"I would if I were you," said Mark.

"Who's that nutty looking chap over by the pool table?" asked Charlie.

Oh, that's Lee," answered Mark, "and, yes, he is as nutty as he looks. He's bloody mad. Keep as far away from him as you can. He starts on people for no reason; he even turns on the screws. He looks a bit of a prick, skinny and scruffy, but I reckon he's dangerous. Even the hard men leave him alone."

"Lock-up" yelled the officer, "behind your doors, lads."

"See ya tomorrow, Mark" said Charlie turning towards his cell.

It was a couple of days later, during association, that Lee approached Mark and Charlie.

"Here comes trouble," whispered Mark.

"Hello lads," began Lee, "this prison, in fact all prisons, are shit. Well, I'm gonna change all that. I'm gonna sort the system for all of you."

Lee sauntered away from the two lads across the ground floor.

"What's he on about?" asked Charlie.

"I ain't got a clue," answered Mark.

A couple of days later Mark and Charlie were sitting on the ground floor when Lee appeared from a cell on the twos. The twos were about thirty feet above the ground floor and a railing ran the length of the second landing to prevent anyone falling, or being pushed, onto the ground floor. Lee went back into the cell and returned into view with a rope made from sheets. One end was fastened round his neck. He tied the other end to the railings.

"He's only gonna jump and hang himself," Charlie said to Mark.

"I wouldn't put it past him" answered Mark, "I told you that he was a bit of a loon."

A crowd had gathered on the ground floor. The noise grew as the tension mounted.

"Go on mate, do us all a favour."

"You ain't got the bottle, you wanker."

"Who's gonna clear-up the mess, you selfish shit."

Lee screeched; then leaped. He didn't waste any time; nobody had a chance to react.

His plan would have worked but for one tiny detail. The rope he'd made from the sheets was too long. He didn't hang in mid-air with a broken neck. No, he crashed to the ground floor and broke both his legs. He was carried from the unit, in agony but very much alive.

"What a nut," said Charlie to Mark, feeling a little relieved, "do you reckon he did that on purpose or do you think that he really intended to die?"

"I'll never be able to work him out," answered Mark, "leave that to the shrinks."

The following day Charlie, Mark and their pal, John, stood chatting on the twos.

"Any of you want to borrow some burn," asked a scarred inmate known as Bull.

"No, we're alright mate," answered Mark.

"Okay," Bull wasn't renowned for long conversation. He walked-off searching for victims.

"You okay for burn then Mark?" asked Charlie.

"Ain't got a single smoke but I wouldn't borrow off people like him."

"Why's that?" asked Charlie.

"Well" said Mark, "when you go to the prison shop you have to pay them back. Double what you borrowed. If you don't they will double the amount again and give you a slap. No, however desperate I was, I wouldn't borrow from them."

"Me neither," said John, "they rely on people being desperate. On the outside I was desperate for a drink and look where it got me. I was so bloody desperate that I robbed three shops with a gun."

"And look at me "thought Charlie to himself, "I was so desperate to get away from old women that I wanted to come to a place like this. A lot of people in here have problems of some sort so I'm not the only one. I do like John and Mark but I would never tell them how I ended-up inside."

Charlie had spent the day in court at Dorking. He had been remanded in custody by that court as well as Esher and Walton Magistrates. Now bail was completely beyond hope. He sat in the cage waiting to be taken to a unit.

"I hope that I go back to Raven," he mused, "as I really would like to stay with Mark and John. Good mates are hard to find - inside or out."

No chance. Partridge unit beckoned.

That night he sat in his cell listening to the arguments taking place out of the windows.

"I don't care what screws are there if you don't give me all your tobacco in the morning I'll fucking batter you."

"He sounds a lovely chap" thought Charlie, as he tried to write a letter to Robert.

Association, the next day, and Charlie was sat on the stairs leading to the twos landing. He was looking at rather than watching a video - he didn't know what it was about. Behind Charlie were a group of rowdy prisoners. They certainly weren't interested in the video, they were looking for trouble and they couldn't have been in a better place than Feltham.

"I don't want to move," thought Charlie, "or I'll look a right wanker. If I stay here am I asking for trouble? I want to avoid trouble if I can, especially with that lot."

Charlie feigned interest in the happenings on the screen. Maybe they would leave him alone.

All of a sudden Charlie felt something on the back of his neck, just above his collar. He soon realised what it was - spittle. One of the bastards had spat at him and, from the feel of it, had struck gold. Quick as a flash he spun around. It was obvious which tosser was responsible.

"If you ignore it, these bastards will never leave you alone," the thought flashed through his mind.

He didn't have time to consider much else. His options were very limited. Stand-up for yourself or become a victim.

Charlie's right hand shot-out and connected sharply with the lad's forehead. Charlie knew, mainly from being in Feltham, the harder you hit the less chance of a reply. He was ready to strike again, he had to be. The lad would fight if he could - he didn't want to look a wimp in front of all his mates. This time, however, the lad was out of luck. He slipped to the floor. He wasn't going to fight so there was no need to hit him again.

"Leave it," Charlie told himself, "you've proved a point and now you don't want to give the others any excuse to join in."

Some chance.

"Very good, pal," said a voice, "I'd like to see what I can do with you. What do you say, you bald bastard? Straights. Just you and me in the dorm."

The youth smiled but something told Charlie he wasn't being friendly.

"What choice have I got," decided Charlie, "I've started so I'll have to try and finish. In for a penny, in for a...... hell of a thrashing."

"Okay mate," he agreed, trying to prevent the fear and reluctance from creeping into his tone.

They both turned and walked into the four man dormitory.

"Here we go," thought Charlie, "this bloke looks confident."

Charlie decided not to jump on his opponent before he turned as he didn't want his mates to join the scrap. He decided to play fair in the hope they would.

"How far we gonna take this?" Charlie asked, trying to break the tension.

"I'm gonna take your fucking head off" snarled the tall, thin skinhead as he whipped out a straight left-hand.

"This shit ain't messing about," decided Charlie, "he wants to bloody kill me. I've been hit by some big blokes, but nothing like this."

Another left hand smashed into Charlie's nose. Charlie hadn't the time to reply. A skilled fighter working-out with a heavyweight oaf - someone who could take a punch but would be unable to hit back.

"I ain't got a prayer like this," Charlie concluded. "If I stand here he'll just keep on working-out with my face."

82

Charlie lunged and grabbed his tall, but toned, opponent. What else could he do?

"Just hold the shit," Charlie urged himself, "as he ain't gonna get bored hitting you. Not with an audience enjoying every punch."

The skinhead's pals were enjoying the one-sided tussle. They were confident of the result.

Charlie clung to the skinhead as if his life depended on it. If it were possible, he'd prefer not to visit the hospital unit.

"You can't just hug him" Charlie reasoned, "got to try and hurt him."

Charlie pulled back his bald head and smashed his forehead into the skinhead's face. Charlie, a fair bit shorter, connected with the lad's mouth. Blood surfaced on the taller lad's lips.

"Better than nothing" thought Charlie, still trying to keep a grip of his opponent.

Charlie held-on. He was not foolish enough to think he had stopped the skinhead. A wounded animal can be a very dangerous thing; especially if its pride is hurt more than anything else.

The lad upped a gear. His injury certainly didn't stop him, in fact it increased his strength and aggression. He struggled, quite easily, from Charlie's desperate clutches and shoved him away. This time the left hand was followed by a right. Charlie's hands failed to protect his face. His nose was not enjoying its best day. Without giving Charlie a chance to move the same combination of blows connected. Charlie was completely unable to protect his face. His head drooped forward as he struggled to stay standing. Two, quite brutal, uppercuts laid Charlie across the dormitory floor - bruised and bloodied.

"I hope that's it," Charlie silently prayed, "he's proved his point and I can't take much more."

Charlie wiped some blood from his eyes and, to his enormous relief, saw the skinhead casually walk from the dormitory.

"I won't try and get-up," thought Charlie, "or he'll probably come back-in and knock me out."

Charlie, totally dazed, could just make-out voices outside the dormitory.

"What a tosser," laughed one of the lads, "still it gave you a nice work-out. Even if it was a bit short."

Charlie lay on the floor. He didn't know what hurt the most - his face or his pride. Not only had he been battered but he was, also, a laughing stock.

"Bastards," he thought, "but I ain't gonna let them destroy me. I'll keep going. I fucking need to be here and I ain't gonna let a bunch of wankers ruin it."

Eventually, Charlie struggled to his feet. The audience had cleared. They had left, well entertained.

"I feel like shit," he pondered, "still I've lived to tell the tale."

A few minutes later and association was over. The inmates waited by their own doors for the wardens to lock them away. The officer who opened Charlie's cell could hardly fail to notice the marks that were visible on his face and the blood splattered on his clothes.

"How was your association, lad?" asked the officer.

"Had better, guv," answered Charlie, "I kept falling over."

"I would get you another shirt, son," said the officer, with a grin. "but they'll probably do you again tomorrow."

Two days later as Charlie sat in his cell he tried to concentrate on a book about serial killers. He heard the jangle of keys. The door opened.

"Court tomorrow, Lloyd, Dorking Magistrates'. Be ready." ordered the warden.

"Okay guv," Charlie replied.

Charlie lay on his bed.

"I can't get bail tomorrow," he thought, "as I'm on remand at Esher and Walton as well as Dorking so I'll be back here tomorrow night. I've been here for about six weeks and, yes, it is crap but I prefer it to the thoughts I was getting outside. I haven't had weird ideas since I've been here. I wonder if I'm cured. Have to wait and see when they do decide to let me out."

Charlie cleaned his teeth, got ready for bed and snuggled under the covers.

"Cured…… cured……" he kept repeating as he drifted off to sleep. All the wonderful things he would do on the outside.

Was he dreaming? Probably.

Chapter 8

Dorking Magistrates' Court hadn't changed. Once again, Charlie was placed in the care of John the Jailer, an officer liked and respected by the prisoner.

"Rob and Kate are already upstairs in the waiting room. They had to answer their bail about twenty minutes ago." John told Charlie, handing the prisoner a cup of tea.

"Thanks guv" said Charlie, taking the cup, "best drink I've had for a while."

"Are you going to plead today?" asked John.

"Guilty as hell" answered the prisoner.

"You won't be going back to Feltham, then," said John, "if you plead guilty they will put you on a Judges' remand…."

"What's that?" asked Charlie.

"Well, that would mean," replied John, "you would be convicted awaiting sentence. No longer on remand. Even though you are on remand at Esher and Walton, you would be sent to a prison from this court."

"Where would I go?" asked Charlie.

"Y.P. wing at Lewes Prison" answered John, "most people who go there say that it's okay."

The three defendants all pleaded guilty. Kate and Robert had their bail conditions extended. Charlie was given a judges' remand.

"Lewes, here I come," thought Charlie, as he left the dock, "at least I ain't gotta go back to that other shit-hole."

As Charlie walked onto the wing in the Victorian jail he was desperate to hide his anxiety.

"This looks like the real thing" he thought, "still the people can't be any worse than at Feltham… can they?"

"Hurry-up, you lot," snapped the short, fat warden, "I haven't got all day."

"The noise is a lot worse than Feltham" thought Charlie, "and I can't stand the stink of stale piss."

"Come on…. Come on" wheezed the warden, "I've got a woman waiting for me. You lot are on the top landing and I haven't got all day."

All the young prisoners were on the top landing, or the fours, as it was commonly called.

"This looks more like a jail," mused Charlie, "this is what you would expect. It looks like trouble, it smells like trouble, it even feels like trouble.... Bloody hell, this place looks shit."

All the cells were for two prisoners. No single cells and no toilets in them. Maybe Feltham wasn't so bad, after all.

Charlie soon met his cell-mate, Steve.

"Shit, he's a big bloke," thought Charlie, as he put his belongings on his bed, "I hope that I get-on with him. He certainly looks a handful. He's mainly muscle. He's got a bit of flab but I ain't gonna tell him, that."

Charlie needn't have worried. Steve was a decent bloke.

"I've been here for a couple of weeks," he told Charlie, "I'm on remand for house burglaries. Don't know how long I'll get. Normally, I wouldn't give a fuck but I do miss my girlfriend, Clare."

Steve talked a great deal about the love of his life.

"I just can't see what a great girl like her sees in somebody like me. She's got a good job...."

"What does she do" interrupted Charlie.

"She looks after nutters," answered Steve, "in a hospital. Once she was clobbered by some geezer who heard voices in his head. She wasn't too bothered. Said that he was ill and needed help. She still works in the same place."

"Heard voices," mused Charlie, "I wonder if I've got something similar. But I've never hit an old woman; I just worry that I might."

"Do you know what was wrong with the bloke?" asked Charlie.

"Schizo... something or other," answered Steve.

"Schizophrenia" suggested Charlie.

"That's the one," agreed Steve, "I knew it was something like that."

"I hope I haven't got that," thought Charlie, "I could have, I suppose, I do hear my bad side making me think that I've battered some old dear."

The more Charlie thought, the more unsure he became. Did he have schizophrenia? Possibly? He bloody hoped not. He just didn't know.

"You okay, mate," Steve's voice burst Charlie's thought bubble.

"Yeah fine," answered Charlie.

"Good" said Steve, "you seemed to be miles away."

"Do you get a lot of trouble in here," enquired Charlie, not wanting to be asked where he had been.

"Well" answered Steve, "you always get the occasional bit of grief in any prison and it ain't no different here. There was a bit of a punch-up at the gym a few days ago. Only a couple of slaps and the two lads were pulled apart."

"I suppose you get that down the local pub on a Friday night," replied Charlie.

"Oh yeah," continued Steve, "I must warn you, my last cell-mate had a little bit of trouble with the lads of the wing."

"What like?" asked Charlie, feeling that he ought to be prepared.

"Well" answered Steve, "he hadn't been here long when the bastards burst in and initiated him."

"What did they do?" asked Charlie.

"They whipped off his trousers and pants and pulled out his pubic hairs with tweezers."

"Bloody hell" commented Charlie, trying to sound casual, "do they initiate everyone?"

"Not sure," said Steve, "they didn't try anything with me."

"I hope that doesn't happen to me," thought Charlie, "it would be so degrading - not to mention fucking painful."

Charlie was worried but he wasn't going to let Steve in on the secret.

"My old bird gives great head" Steve changed the subject.

It was during second slop-out, a day or so later, that Charlie was reminded where he was. He still hadn't got used to the chamber pots used in Lewes - he definitely preferred Feltham's toilet habits. He sat on his bed reading a book about a borstal's regime - at least he could compare it to present day. A slight noise attracted his attention. He shot a glance towards the cell door. It wasn't Steve returning. Four hostile prisoners stood by the door, which had been almost closed. The five of them were out of sight from the rest of the prison. Anyway, who cared what happened to a prisoner in cell thirty-four, landing four, A wing?

"Mustn't let this happen," Charlie told himself as he clambered to his feet. He tried to stop shaking; at least he tried not to let them see he was shaking.

He turned slowly and faced the group. They all looked serious - surely there were more important things in life that degrading someone. What pleasure did people get from humiliating others for no reason?

"There's no point in pleading with them" decided Charlie, "people like this don't show mercy as it makes them seem weak."

The cells, being fairly narrow owing to their layout, forced the gang to approach their intended victim in single file.

"I've got half a chance in such a small area" thought Charlie, "half a chance not to get my pubes pulled-out with some tweezers."

The biggest member of the group stepped forward.... cautiously. A tall lad, quite well built with swept-back blonde hair. Rugged, but good-looking. A small tattoo of an eagle covered the left side of his neck.

"He's the type of bloke that I'd expect to see chatting-up the local lovely in a club" thought Charlie. "Ain't it amazing what goes through your mind in times of stress?"

Charlie decided what action had to be taken. As eagle-neck stretched-out, Charlie grabbed a coffee jar. He smashed it, with as much strength as he could muster, into the lower part of the offender's face.

"I couldn't give a shit what the damage is," decided Charlie, "I ain't gonna be degraded by some pretty boy."

A scream, more of a yelp, followed the cracking sound. Eagle-neck writhed slightly on the floor... groaning.

"Thank fuck for that," thought Charlie, standing over the wounded inmate.

The other three eyed the coffee jar still in Charlie's hand. The jar remained intact.

"You don't want a try, do you?" Charlie spoke softly. He didn't feel the need to shout. He had made a point.

"Alright mate, we're leaving" said the next-in-line, a short fat chap with a very pointed nose, "we ain't got a problem....... just forget it."

The posse helped their injured companion from the cell leaving behind a very relieved inmate.... in a state of shock. Charlie struggled to gain some self-control. He mustn't lose the plot now. The hard bit had been done.

"I don't reckon they'll be back" thought Charlie, "after all, there's plenty of easier meat in here."

Charlie quickly settled into Lewes' fairly relaxed regime.

"I prefer this place to Feltham," he mused, "less trouble; not so many vicious little shits."

Each day, about mid-morning, Charlie would go to the gymnasium to train with the weights. It was either pumping iron, playing football, walking round the yard or sitting in the cell. Charlie looked forward to his daily exercise routine.

Charlie was working on his biceps with a fellow inmate, Sean.

"What you done, to get stuck in here?" asked Charlie, while the two of them took a break from training.

"Had a scrap outside a boozer," answered Sean, a muscular man with jet-black hair, "only hit the bloke once and here I am."

"Must have done some damage," said Charlie.

"Well yeah," answered Sean, "it was a good punch. Matey had to have his nose totally rebuilt. Apparently, his hooter was completely shattered. He just stood there, shitting himself, and let me hit him - what did he expect?"

"Did you try for bail?" asked Charlie.

"Sure did," replied Sean, "but the bastards said that I was likely to interfere with witnesses. It's bloody stupid, in the army you can have a fight without the worry of being nicked."

"Did you like the army," asked Charlie.

"Best life there is, mate," replied Sean, a grin covering his tanned complexion, "you can't beat it."

Sean grasped the bar and, slowly, curled the first of his ten repetitions.

"I wouldn't want to get on the wrong side of him," thought Charlie, as he watched the stockily-built young man strain to finish the set.

Back in the gym, one rainy Tuesday morning, Charlie and Sean grunted and groaned trying to complete sets of bench press. Sean found it a lot easier than his training partner, his chest was probably the most powerful part of his body.

On the adjacent bench, three black inmates weren't working very hard on their muscular development. They were laughing and joking and it became extremely obvious to Charlie that the lads were trying to mock him and his partner.

"I wish they'd shut-up" thought Charlie, "if Sean realises they're taking the piss, there's gonna be trouble. I'll have to get involved and I could really do without it."

Sean stared at the black lads then….. looked away.

"Shit," thought Charlie, "maybe he doesn't want any trouble." Some hope.

Sean, once again, turned towards the trio.

"Want to sort it out?" he almost spat the words.

Silence. They all looked at each other.

"You in, Charlie?" he asked, turning to his mate.

"If it kicks-off and you need me, I am" was the reluctant reply.

Charlie carried-on bench pressing the weighted bar.

Sean didn't train. He stood staring at the black lads. He was saving his energy and, at the same time, showing them he was not one to be crossed.

Charlie felt a familiar build-up of anxiety.

"I hope that it doesn't start," he thought, "but Sean seems the type of bloke who won't let it go. I can't bottle-it and let down a mate."

"Right," bellowed the gym orderly, "time's up. Go and get yourselves a shower, you smelly bastards." Charlie and Sean watched, silently, as the other young offenders filed out of the gym towards the changing rooms. The black lads were near the front of the group. They didn't even glance in Sean's direction.

"They've lost their nerve," thought Charlie, "they don't want to know. Good. I hope Sean will see this as a moral victory and leave it alone."

Sean hadn't spoken. Charlie looked at his pal's face and didn't see the expression of a man happy with a moral victory.

Sean headed towards the changing rooms with an angry stride. Charlie followed. He had taken this path and now he had to see where it would finish.

Sean went into the changing area and headed straight towards one of the trio.

"He's made up his mind," decided Charlie, "I suppose he might be trying to scare the lad, but I doubt it."

"Alright mate," said the lad with a half-hearted attempt at a smile.

Sean didn't reply. The right hand was fast, very fast. Charlie, who was standing right behind Sean, didn't see much until the clenched fist smashed into the lad's face. The black offender, who hadn't even had time to get-up from his seat, knew he'd been hit. His head smashed into the wall behind him as his nose shattered from the power and accuracy of the blow.

"Bloody hell" mumbled Charlie, "I can see how Sean caused so much damage to the poor shit outside the pub."

One of the others decided he really should stand by his pal. He started to clamber to his feet.

"Brave man" thought Charlie, "but I don't reckon he fancies his chances, just being loyal. I wonder what the price of loyalty will be for him."

The price was a left hook. The punch smashed into the side of the man's face. At least it was all over quickly. The black lad slumped back onto his seat; he'd had more than enough.

The third lad had less loyalty….. or more sense. He wasn't going to get involved and moved away from the action.

"Bloody hell" thought Charlie, "that was easy. I'm glad that me and Sean are pals."

Thursday afternoons were for watching a video. This Thursday was no different. During the video some inmates would be called for a visit. They would then be taken by the officer to the visiting hall to see their friend, family or loved one.

"I might have a visit this afternoon" Charlie whispered to Steve, "I sent my sister details about visiting
days ago."

"I hope you do, mate," replied Steve, "it's always nice to see someone from the outside."

Today's film was a comedy. The star of the show was a policeman who had little idea how to do the job. A complete idiot, in fact.

"Wish I'd had that wanker on my case," whispered Steve, "I certainly wouldn't have ended-up in this hole."

"I know what you mean," replied Charlie, although he was sure most constables would have little trouble with him. He craved the security of prison.

"I suppose that I wanted to be nicked," thought Charlie, "and if a criminal wants to go to prison that's usually where he ends-up. I was reckless about getting caught; a part of me really hoped for the day when the police came knocking on the door."

Charlie hadn't noticed the warden on visits standing at the back of the room. He was miles away in his private world of strange behaviour.

"Baxter, Pearce, Wright and Lloyd. Come with me."

Charlie snapped back into reality. He had a visit. Time to mix with the outside world - if only temporarily.

Charlie strolled along the rows of tables in the visiting room. It was a large room with many people and Charlie felt awkward; was everyone looking at him?

"Why would anyone care what you are doing?" he told himself, "they've got more important things to worry about."

Eventually, he sank into a chair opposite his sister.

"Hello" began Charlie, "how's it going?"

"Oh, things are okay," replied Lucy. "Am I your first visitor?"

"You sure are," said Charlie, "you know it's really strange seeing you in this place."

"Why's that?"

"Well" answered Charlie, "a familiar face in here. It just feels weird."

"So, what's it like?" asked Lucy.

"Well, it's not too bad. The people are okay. I prefer it in here than in Feltham. There was always so much trouble in there. I ain't sure what they put in the food but for the first couple of weeks I just couldn't have a shit."

"Have you been beaten-up yet?" asked Lucy, with a half-smile.

"Lots of grief in Feltham and a bit here. Everyone gets some shit in prison - it doesn't matter who you are."

Lucy nodded. Fascinated by a world she would hate to experience.

"Have you seen Rob, Kate or Jane?" asked Charlie.

"Not a lot," said Lucy, "they don't come round very much anymore."

"Probably don't want to see Hazel" said Charlie.

"I suppose so," replied Lucy.

"Anyway, how is Hazel?" asked Charlie.

"She's alright. She doesn't mention you very often. When her friends ask where you are she just tells them that you are away and leaves it at that."

"Oh right," said Charlie, unsure of a suitable comment.

The visit flew passed. There was much catching-up to be done.

"Finish your visit now, please," said an officer, tapping Charlie gently on the back.

"Okay guv."

Charlie turned back to his sister.

"Right Lou," he said, "come back as soon as you can and, if you want, bring Edward or Richard. I'll write to you tonight. Oh yeah, tell Hazel that I'll see her soon."

"See you soon" said Lucy, standing-up.

Charlie headed towards the door that took him back onto the wing. Back to a different world. A separate world; separated from Lucy, Hazel, Jane, Rob......all the people he had known before his liberty was removed.

Charlie's arms swung freely as he paced across the visiting room. His mind was elsewhere. He was in the pub with Edward, playing football in the garden with Rob and shopping with Lucy. Of course, the shops had everything he wanted and he had more than enough money. The outside world seemed so perfect when you were in prison.

From the corner of his eye, Charlie noticed a stooped old lady as she struggled to her feet with the much needed aid of a walking stick. He couldn't really fail to notice, he had just strolled past her.

"Oh shit, oh no" he thought, "did I hit her?"

He stared at the elderly woman - she appeared unharmed. No worse than she had been before Charlie passed-by. He carried-on walking towards the door.

"The idea of me hitting her came from nowhere," he reasoned, "there was no warning; it was just there."

"You didn't hit her," he tried to reassure himself, as his heartbeat pounded wildly.

Charlie reached the door. At least, now, he could return to the wing.

As he walked along the landing to his cell his mind was working overtime.

"What the fuck is happening to me?" thought Charlie.

"Did you punch the old biddy?" he asked himself.

"No," he answered, "I'm sure I didn't."

"So what's the problem?" he continued to grief himself.

"The fact is," he held a conversation inside his head, "I got a worry from these bloody thoughts while I'm in prison."

"You were on a visit," he told himself, "so there was a chance of meeting an old woman. Look, if going on a visit is going to be a problem then I won't take any visits."

Charlie pushed open his cell door and walked inside. The cell was empty. He sat down on his bed and put his head in his hands. He was upset about the irrational thought, to say the least.

"Fuck. Fuck. Fuck. Bastard thoughts." he murmured, "I just hope they don't find a way onto the wing."

"How the hell can they?" he asked himself, "I'm sure that you won't meet any old women on the young prisoners' wing of a male prison."

"I hope that you're right," he carried on the conversation in his head, "but as far as these bloody thoughts are concerned I wouldn't like to take anything for granted."

It was while before Charlie had regained his control. When he felt able he picked-up a book and tried to concentrate on the words in front of him.

The days passed. People went to court; some returned, others didn't. Soon it was Charlie's turn to appear before the magistrates. He left Lewes in a prison van, not entirely sure what to expect.

Chapter 9

Charlie sat in the cell underneath the courts.

"I wonder what will happen today," he thought, "will I go free to deal with the thoughts? I doubt they've improved because I had problems in the visiting room at the prison. So, they could have got worse. I suppose it doesn't matter what happens - if I go back to prison I'll have a bit more time to sort-out my head but if they let me out I can see how the thoughts bother me and if they are too bad I'll get myself put back in."

Charlie didn't have a great deal of time to think. John the jailer opened the door after a few minutes.

"Come on, Charlie," he said, "your turn."

Charlie stood in the dock. Robert and Kate were on the opposite side of the spacious courtroom staring at him. They didn't have to stand in the dock as they were on bail. Would they find-out what it was like to be led from the court to the cells below?

The trio's solicitor soon got the proceedings underway.

"I put it to you, Sir, that the offences, although numerous, are at the less serious end of the scale.

Charlie Lloyd was the self-confessed ringleader and admits that he had to persuade my other clients to take part. It is most likely that these offenders would never have appeared before a criminal court had it not been for Mr. Lloyd. They have behaved themselves whilst on bail and I would strongly urge you, Sir, not to expose them to custody for even a short period of time. I believe a community sentence would be much more appropriate."

"Blimey," thought Charlie, "is this bloke trying to get those two out of it and use me as a scapegoat? I'm going get ages. Maybe I should have got a different brief. Still, at least, I can control the bloody thoughts while I'm inside. I wonder if Robert and Kate would have been so keen to do all the jobs with me if they had known my true reasons. They are standing here today, with a serious threat of prison, and they still don't know why I was so keen to get them involved with crime."

Charlie's attention was grabbed by his solicitor's voice.

"Mr. Lloyd, for his part, admits his guilt. He has spent a while in custody and has learnt a hard lesson. In future, he will strive to keep away from crime and involving others in his dishonest ways."

"If the thoughts would just fuck-off" mused Charlie, "then, yes, I would try very hard to lead an honest life."

Charlie glanced at the solicitor who was still trying to convince the magistrates not to give Charlie a custodial sentence.

"As Mr. Lloyd has spent a period in custody I would respectfully suggest that, as a last chance, he is given a punishment other than imprisonment."

"Good speech, mate," mumbled Charlie, glancing at his solicitor, "you certainly gave it a good try."

The prosecution took the floor. He described the burglaries and thefts with which the trio had been charged. He certainly wasn't going to forget Charlie's stolen truck.

"The other two defendants charged in relation to the driving away of the truck are being dealt with separately," he concluded.

"Thank-you" said the magistrate as he and his colleagues retired.

"Well" thought Charlie, "it's up to them now. I hope they got a little bit last night."

Charlie felt anxious - he simply couldn't help himself. The familiar symptoms grew inside him. As much as he tried to fight his increasing heartbeat, perspiring palms and fidgeting hands, he just couldn't.

"What does it matter," he told himself, "whatever happens I will still have problems. If I go to prison I'll have to put-up with that and if they let me out I'll have those bloody thoughts. So, one way or another, I'll be pissed-off."

He looked up. His eyes met with Rob and Kate. He gave them a cheeky grin and shrugged his shoulders.

"I don't want them to think I'm bothered," thought Charlie, "I want them to think I couldn't give a shit. I can see they both look terrified but I hope they can't read inside my head."

The magistrates returned.

"I need the loo" panicked Charlie, "I hope they make it quick or I could be caught short."

"Stand-up please, Mr. Lloyd" the tone was solemn, the eyes intent, "we have listened very carefully to your solicitor but we still feel only custody would be appropriate in your case owing to the number of offences and a complete disregard of bail conditions. You will go to a young offenders' institution for six months."

"That could have been a lot worse," reasoned Charlie, "taking off time on remand, I'll be free in a couple of weeks. That'll give me a bit of time to sort-out my head before I get out."

Charlie gave a thumbs-up to Rob and Kate. Robert looked like he was about to throw-up, collapse or both. John took Charlie back down the stairs to the cells.

"Rob looks in a bit of a state," said John.

"I reckon he'll need a doctor not a jailer if he gets put-away," answered Charlie.

"Right Charlie," said John, "I'd better get back into court in case Rob or Kate are joining you."

"What do you reckon they'll get?" asked Charlie.

"Soon see," said John, closing the door.

Charlie waited. It wasn't long before he heard footsteps. John opened the door - he was alone.

"What happened to them?" asked Charlie.

"Both the same - two hundred and forty hours community service and two years probation."

"Bet Rob was relieved," said Charlie.

"Just a bit."

It wasn't long before Charlie was on his way back to Lewes.

"Bit of a result today," decided Charlie, "free in a couple of weeks and I've always got the option to go back if I can't cope."

Charlie soon got to know his cellmate, Craig. They chatted and laughed - Craig was always cheerful.

"Don't reckon I'd be that happy if I was looking at eight years," thought Charlie, "but I suppose I might have to get myself sent back if I can't cope with the bloody thoughts. I certainly ain't gonna tell Craig why I went into crime; he'll think I'm a right weirdo. He's a junkie - that's why he did armed robberies - but that's pretty normal in here."

A couple of days after arriving in Lewes Charlie had just finished slopping-out. He strolled back to his cell nodding at a few familiar faces. He pushed the door and walked inside. He looked at Craig, his eyes couldn't fail to notice - Craig's face was covered in blood.

"What the fuck's happened to you?" yelled Charlie, "who done this?"

Craig didn't speak. He stood still - blood dripping.

Charlie dropped his chamber pot and walked towards Craig. Something wasn't right. He caught sight of something placed on the table. A razor blade. A bloodied razor blade. Craig's own razor blade.

"Nobody's been here," said Charlie, "have they? You done this to yourself."

Charlie handed Craig the nearest towel. As Craig dabbed gently on his face Charlie noticed the lad's arm - he slashed at that into the bargain.

The blood soaked into the towel. The actual cuts were very superficial - no stitches would be needed. The main problem was Craig's mental state. The chances were that he would do something similar in the not too distant future.

"You'll keep it quiet, won't you" Craig was almost pleading, "no need to tell anyone."

"I won't tell a soul," said Charlie, "as long as it ain't gonna happen again."

Craig sat on his bed. He looked a sorry state.

"Why did you do it, mate?" asked Charlie gently.

"Pissed-off with it all, I guess," answered Craig, "gonna be away for ages and I ain't got nothing to look forward to. Felt low, depressed, thought it might change things."

They chatted for a while until Craig, face and arm badly scratched, fell asleep.

Charlie lay on his own bed staring into the surrounding darkness.

"Who'd have thought it?" he reflected on the evening's events, "Craig always seemed so happy. Nothing seemed to bother him. Just goes to show you can't judge a book by its cover.

I wonder how bad the thoughts would have to get to make me do something like that? The bastard things do make me angry, a bit depressed sometimes, but I hope I can always keep a grip on things even if I have to live in prison."

Charlie rolled onto his stomach and gazed at the bars on the tiny window.

"Maybe it's this place," he wondered, "maybe after a while it sends you potty. I mean, I know I'll be out soon but how would I feel if I had to do a few years?"

Charlie's thoughts seemed to wander gradually into the distance. Sleep was very nearly upon him.

Days passed, little changed except the prisoners. Out with the old, in with the new.

Charlie was reading in his cell. He liked to read in prison, he could lose himself in someone else's world. It had to be better than his.

Officer Bradley opened the door.

"You're off to Hollesley Bay tomorrow, Lloyd. First thing. Okay?"

Having said his piece the warden closed the door without giving Charlie a chance to reply. Too bad if it wasn't okay.

"You lucky bastard" said Craig, "I wish I was going there."

"What's it like then?" asked Charlie.

"It's an open nick. No fences. They leave you there on trust. You could walk out at any time if you wanted. Lots of lads go to the local village to work. Not much trouble, either. Most of the lads are doing short stretches and they ain't done nothing violent."

"Are you having me on?" asked Charlie.

"No mate," answered Craig, "I am being totally straight with you."

"I'll write to you when I'm there," said Charlie.

"Make sure you do."

Hollesley Bay was clusters of modern buildings set in large, well tended grounds. Outside the institution were fields, trees and woods.

The prison van drove through the countryside and a small village before arriving at the low security institution.

"This place is certainly out in the sticks," thought Charlie, catching sight of some farm animals in a distant field, "the only fences are to keep the animals from coming in, not to stop us lot from getting out."

As trainee KRO655 Lloyd walked to his unit an officer went past - on a bicycle.

"Fuck me," murmured Charlie to himself, "this place takes the piss."

Once on the unit Charlie was shown to his room. He arranged his kit and waited to join the other trainees for tea.

"This ain't too bad," decided Charlie, "I reckon I should just keep my head down and finish my sentence."

Charlie soon settled. He was given a job as a wing cleaner. Not a trusted position, like working in the local village, but not too bad for somebody who was soon to be going home.

Charlie, a couple of days after his arrival, was in the washroom cleaning his teeth. He felt good, he felt alive, he was in open conditions and seemed to be coping.

"I hope the thoughts are a thing of the past," he silently prayed as he scrubbed at his teeth, "maybe I've learnt to cope better since I've been away."

Charlie soon became aware of a small group of trainees standing behind him. They weren't washing, they weren't brushing their teeth or shaving and they weren't using the toilets. They were, simply, watching him.

"Shit," thought Charlie, "why the fuck are they watching me clean my teeth? They want something and it ain't tips on better brushing."

"Has mummy told you to check behind your ears?" the ringleader, a tall lad with cropped dark hair, was obviously looking for trouble.

Charlie opted not to rise to the bait.

"If I say nothing, then they might leave it alone," he thought, brushing slightly quicker than before.

The same trainee rolled-up his sleeves displaying his brightly tattooed arms.

"I reckon he's scared" he jeered, "probably in here for being a sex case."

"Just can't let this go" decided Charlie, "better to have a go now than leave it. This lot would be on my case morning, noon and night."

Charlie slowly turned to face the lad. In prison it's very hard to turn the other cheek.

"Look mate," he spoke quite calmly under the circumstances, "I ain't looking for trouble, so piss-off and leave me alone."

"Oh, quite the 'ard man" mocked the lad, giving Charlie a sudden shove.

Charlie stepped back to maintain his balance.

"What now" he thought, "do I attack or let that go? I ain't got long in here so would it be best to walk-away?"

He held the gaze of the taller lad.

"You could spend most of your life in and out of prison with your problems so you can't start behaving like a mug" decided Charlie.

Charlie dropped his gaze. The tall lad seemed to relax. He looked pleased - point proved. He let his hands fall to his sides.

"Here goes," decided Charlie, glancing at the open target.

His right hand came from his side and landed on the taller lad's hooked nose. Direct hit. A little blood oozed, Charlie had been hoping for more. Hook Nose swayed but kept standing. Charlie's left hand swung but failed to connect. This gave Captain Hook the time to recover. He banged a savage right-hand into Charlie's stomach. Charlie, with the wind taken from his sails, grabbed the lanky Captain hook. He knew only too well if he didn't hang-on he would be slaughtered.

The other two lads watched the tussle. They appeared confident of the result.

"You're fucking dead," growled Hook, trying to free an arm from Charlie's grasp.

Nobody realised that an additional person had joined the audience.

"What the hell is going on here?" roared the officer.

Charlie, Hook and the other lads turned around. The senior officer looked far from amused.

"We was only mucking about, sir," said Hook.

"Course you were, Robinson" said the warden.

"It's true, guv" added Charlie, hoping the officer would fail to notice the blood on Hook's shirt.

"Both of you will see the governor first thing in the morning" snapped the screw, "now get back to your rooms."

"Shit," thought Charlie, as he left the washroom, "just what I didn't want. Still there ain't no point crying over spilt milk."

The screw hammered on Charlie's door to inform the lad that it was time to be out of bed. As Charlie struggled from his pit he could hear the officer further down the dormitory.

"Governor's Report today," thought Charlie, as he struggled to make his bed-pack. "I wonder if I'll get extra days. Probably will. Still you have to have a fight in prison and sometimes you are going to get caught."

When Charlie had made his bed-pack and tidied his room he walked to the dining area. He slumped into the chair next to his mate, Andy.

"Got to see the Governor today," he whispered to Andy, a quiet lad who only spoke to a few of the other inmates.

"Why's that then?" asked Andy.

"Bit of grief with Robinson and his pals."

"Robinson's always causing trouble," said Andy, "best to keep away from him."

"He just started," said Charlie.

"Yeah, he often does. He'll probably have to serve nearly all of his eighteen months."

"What's he in here for?" asked Charlie.

"Stealing top of the range motors."

"How long have you got to go, Andy?" questioned Charlie.

"I'm out in a couple of months," replied Andy, "and, believe me, I will never steal again. Two years has certainly taught me a lesson."

Charlie didn't finish his breakfast. He wouldn't have admitted it but he was a little concerned about seeing the Governor.

"Couldn't give a toss," he lied to Andy,

"Ain't you out soon?" said Andy.

"Meant to be," replied Charlie, "but I shouldn't think that I will be after this morning."

Mr. Collins, a senior officer, strolled into the dining area and cleared his throat. Silence fell, almost immediately.

"Sinton, Hamilton, Lloyd, Robinson, Barford, Neale and Mason - to see the Governor. The rest of you report for work."

"Good luck, mate," murmured Andy, leaving the table.

The seven unlucky trainees marched to the segregation unit, or the block as it was better known, accompanied by two wardens. They would be held under lock and key in separate cells until it was their turn to see the governor.

"I wonder what I'll get," thought Charlie, sitting on the stone floor, "might have to stay in here 'til discharge. Oh well, I'll soon know."

The cell door creaked as it opened.

"Okay Lloyd, your turn. The Governor is ready for you."

The Governor's office was like a miniature courtroom. Charlie sat in the place of the defendant and listened to the evidence.

"Is there anything you would like to say in your defence before I pass sentence?" asked the Governor, after listening to his officer describe what he had seen in the washroom.

"Well, yes Sir," answered Charlie, trying to be cool, calm and collective, "we weren't fighting, we were just messing about. I realise now that this was a very stupid thing to be doing and I do see how it might have looked to the officer."

The governor gazed directly at the tense young man. Charlie's schooldays flashed through his mind.

"Yourself and Robinson have both given a similar version of events so I am going to sentence you for skylarking. You will lose seven days remission. You may return to the unit."

"Thank-you, Sir," said Charlie, standing-up.

"Shit," he thought, "trust my luck. Fucking wanker."

It was a Thursday morning and Charlie, on hands and knees, was scrubbing the dining room floor. Peter and Phil, the other cleaners, were busy in the washrooms. Nobody else was around. Charlie reached behind him for his bucket. Nothing harmful in that, or so you would believe.

"Was an old woman behind me," Charlie panicked, "did I hit her when I stretched-out my arm?"

105

Charlie turned his head. No-one was there - no trainees, no screws and, certainly, no old women.

"What if you hit her and she's managed to stagger away?" Charlie's inner voice questioned.

This idea was so ridiculous that it should have been comical. Not to Charlie. He was far from laughing.

"There's not going to be an old lady watching you clean the floor in prison, is there?" he tried to reassure himself.

"What's to stop some old dear wandering into this room?" Charlie inner voice would try anything to escalate the concern.

"Fuck this. Fuck cleaning this fucking floor." growled Charlie, sitting on his bottom in the middle of the dining area. Head in hands.

Charlie felt worried, then angry. He was worried he'd hurt an old woman, and then angry as, once again, he'd been worried.

His heart-beat pumped. His eyes failed to focus. He had perspiration on his hands and face. He replayed the moment time and time again.

"You certainly didn't hit anyone," he told himself.

As time passed the inner voice of doubt grew weaker. He realised he had had another thought put into his head and that was all it was, a thought.

"You alright, Charlie," said Phil, back from the washrooms, "you seem miles away."

"Just dreaming, mate," answered Charlie, trying to sound cheerful. He felt like crap.

The intrusive thought was never far from Charlie's mind. He just wanted the day to end. He wanted to be put in his room for the night so that he could devise a plan of action.

It seemed like a ten stretch but, eventually, Charlie lay in his bed staring at a picture on the wall. After his day, it was unlikely that he would be rescued by sleep for a long while.

"What the hell am I going to do?" he asked himself, "now the thoughts get me in visiting rooms, open conditions…. Where will it end it all end?

The girl in the picture was smiling. At least someone was happy.

"Right," Charlie murmured into the covers, "it's simple. When you get out of here you see how the thoughts are. If they are too bad then you get yourself sent back to Lewes on remand. Refuse to see anyone on a visit and you'll be fine. If, when you've been sentenced, they put you in an open nick, just runaway. When they get you, it will be a closed prison. Bingo."

"Not much of a life, is it?" he said to himself.

"It'll have to do for now. Needs must and all that."

The last few days ran smoothly. No worries and no hassle. Robinson had obviously found another target. The thoughts obviously hadn't found the right moment.

"Take care, Andy. Don't let the bastards wear you down." said Charlie, before he went to his room for the last time.

Early the following morning Charlie walked-out of Hollesley Bay, a free agent.

"Yes," he thought, "I am free from this place but I am still trapped by my own mind."

Chapter 10

Charlie paced along the rows of parked cars.

"No old women in sight," he thought, "I might be okay."

He soon saw a white metro with Lucy sat in the driver's seat, grinning.

"Hello Charlie," she said, as he opened the door, "glad to be out?"

"Feels good," answered Charlie.

Charlie looked at the young man in the passenger seat.

"Hello Charlie," he said, "long time, no see."

"Eh," began Charlie.

"This is Jason," offered Lucy, "I thought you knew him."

"Yeah, of course," said Charlie, climbing into the back of the vehicle, "how are you doing?"

Charlie, although he didn't know Jason very well, liked what he had seen.

"So far, so good" thought Charlie, "maybe the thoughts will leave me alone. With everything going on I could be alright."

The car began the journey home; three hours would be a good run.

"So what was it like in there?" asked Jason, "were there a lot of fights?"

"Bits of trouble," answered Charlie, "but it's not really as bad as you would expect."

"What do you mean?" pressed Jason.

"Well, there were a few scraps but I didn't see anyone getting shagged in the showers."

"I wouldn't want to go in there," said Jason.

"Don't blame you, mate."

It was an hour into the journey, on the motorway, when a car appeared from nowhere. The driver must have pulled out of a slip road without looking. Lucy didn't stand a chance. Both vehicles sustained minor damage but, fortunately, nobody was hurt. Jason was out the car like a ferret up a drainpipe.

"What's your problem, mate," he yelled, striding towards the other vehicle.

Charlie, slower to react, followed behind.

An elderly gentleman, bespectacled and bald, struggled from the driver's side. The old lady, on the passenger's side, made no attempt to leave her seat. Charlie looked at her. He felt slightly weaker than he had before the incident.

"Don't panic," he urged himself, "she's not going to leave the car. If she does get out I'll just walk away. Nothing's going to kick-off so Jason won't need me."

Charlie watched, still a little uncomfortable, as Jason walked towards the old driver.

Charlie hurried to catch his sister's boyfriend.

"No point starting anything" he said, placing a hand on Jason's arm, "it was an accident and they're very old."

The old chap admitted responsibility so Jason and Charlie retired and let Lucy sort-out the details.

Their car was towed to a local garage. Lucy, with little choice, phoned a taxi.

"What a bloody good start," laughed Charlie, as they waited for their taxi.

Lucy and Jason chatted about the accident.

"That was okay," thought Charlie, "I coped quite well. Okay, I felt a bit strange when I saw the old girl but I didn't get any horrible thoughts. If I don't get any worse, I could manage with life out here."

After listening to a taxi driver who doubled as a comedian for two hours Jason, Lucy and Charlie arrived home.

"Thank the Lord for that," thought Charlie, as he walked into the house, "home and no worries."

Hazel was pleased to see her son but had no desire to hear about his recent experiences.

After a refreshing soak in a hot bath Charlie, dressed in denim dungarees, joined the others in the kitchen.

"How's Edward" Charlie asked Lucy, keen to know about his pal.

"Still getting into trouble. He's in court soon for burglary or fighting - I think."

"I reckon I'll phone him and see what he's doing."

Charlie and Edward had a brief chat and arranged to meet in a local pub.

"You'll love it there," concluded Edward, "plenty of talent."

"See you later," said Charlie.

Charlie didn't take long to decide what to wear - denim dungarees.

"I hope I'm okay in a lively place - don't want to get any horrible thoughts. Still Edward and the others will know if I do anything bad so, if I'm still worried about something in the morning, I can ask them what happened" he decided.

By the time Charlie was ready to leave he was sure that he would have a wonderful night.

As Charlie entered the pub, he felt intimidated by the number of people, the loud music and the atmosphere. Nevertheless, it didn't take him too long to spot Edward's muscular frame in the crowd. Edward was drinking with four friends. Charlie was fairly close to all of them. Richard, a burly lad with long dark hair, liked a scrap. He had come close to prison but had been lucky, so far. Jane, Charlie's partner in many crimes, was delighted to see one of her closest pals. Mandy, attractive with finely chiselled features and ripe body, was fascinated by crime but would never participate. And Clare, plump and good for a laugh, was the type of girl who looked really good after a few pints.

"Alright, you lot," yelled Charlie, so he was heard over the general babble.

They all seemed quite pleased to see their pal. After a couple of quick pints Charlie was able to match their conversation - unabridged crap spouted from all directions.

"Great tattoo you've had done, Ed" said Charlie, staring at the red dagger on Edward's neck.

"Couple of weeks ago, mate," replied Edward, staring at Charlie's hands, "what about you then?"

"There's fuck all to do in your cell," replied Charlie, "something to pass the time."

Meanwhile, Richard appeared to be trying his luck with Mandy.

"I've fancied you for ages," he purred, moving closer.

Mandy whispered in his ear. Richard moved his arm from the chair and draped it around her feminine shoulders.

"I bet it was frustrating in there, eh, Chaz?" said Edward, turning to Charlie.

"You ain't wrong," replied his mate, "I dreamt of a trim, sensual body."

"Well, tonight could be your lucky night," said Edward, an air of confidence in his tone.

"Drink always has that effect, still he ain't completely wrecked," reasoned Charlie, glancing around the pub.

"What about those two?" suggested Charlie, indicating a couple of uglier specimens.

"What the fuck are you on?" shrieked Edward, "I ain't that fucking desperate."

"They ain't too bad," said Charlie.

"Don't be so bloody stupid - I'd rather shag you."

Charlie had a few pints. Edward knocked back pint after pint as if he needed alcohol to live.

As Edward sunk his tenth or eleventh drink he lent across to his mate.

"You know what, Chaz? Those two old tarts ain't too bad. In fact, I could probably show them one hell of a time."

"I bet you could, mate," Charlie, desperate beyond hope, encouraged.

"There'll be knocked sideways when we make our move, Chaz,"

"You ain't wrong," said Charlie, "come on, let's see what we can do."

Charlie walked and Edward staggered across the lounge bar keeping their sights on the intended targets.

"Hi" began Edward, "I'm Ed and this is my mate, Chaz."

"Are you?" replied one of the young ladies, the accent extremely posh.

Edward appeared bemused. They should be keen at the very least. They must want him. Didn't all women find him desirable?

"You don't reckon their together do you, Chaz? whispered Edward.

"Eh?" mumbled Charlie.

"You know….. lesbians."

"No, I doubt it," answered Charlie, "keep your voice down."

Edward stood in front of the ladies, swaying slightly.

"So what are your names?" tried Charlie, trying to salvage pride at the very least.

"I'm Sue and this is Sarah," answered Sue, a stumpy girl with severe acne.

"Mind if we sit down" ventured Charlie, encouraged by this slight success.

"If you really must," snapped Sarah, a tall female with a nice figure, completely ruined by an elephantine nose.

"We're in here, Chaz," murmured Edward, a little too loudly.

The two ladies glanced at each other, eyebrows raised.

The awkward foursome sat in silence. Sue and Sarah looking bored. Edward, gulping his pint, looking pissed and Charlie, dragging on a fag, looking embarrassed.

"I'm just going to the toilet, excuse me," said Sue.

Edward finished his pint. He stood carefully, and then wobbled to the bar. When he got back to the silent Sarah and the cringing Charlie there was still no sign of Sue.

"Sue must have gone for a number two," slurred Ed, sitting in her seat.

"So, what line of work are you in?" asked Charlie, looking at Sarah.

"I'm a secretary," she replied.

"Good fun?" tried Charlie.

"Okay," she answered.

Charlie admitted defeat. If they wouldn't talk to them, it was highly unlikely they would sleep with them.

Sue, eventually, reappeared.

"Must have got tired of hiding in the bogs," thought Charlie, "probably rather listen to our shit that smell everyone else's."

"Wonderful," she snapped, seeing Edward slumped in her place, "now I've nowhere to sit."

"As long as I've got a face, you'll always have somewhere to sit," slurred Ed.

Sue and Sarah looked shocked - rather offended, in fact.

"I beg your pardon" began Sue.

"Oh God" thought Charlie, "had more chance of a shag in prison."

Charlie stood up.

"Come on, Edward, I think that Jane wants us," he said.

Charlie and Edward left the table and headed towards their pals.

"Thank the Lord for that," murmured Sue.

"I reckon I could have scored there," slurred Ed, "how could two old dogs like that say no to anything with a pulse."

Charlie left Edward with Jane and the others and headed towards the bar.

"Well," he thought, "I didn't score but, on a happier note, I didn't get any of those bloody intrusive thoughts. So far, so good. Although a shag would have been very welcome."

Charlie struggled back towards his group, desperately trying not to spill the non-alcoholic drinks.

"I reckon Ed should knock the booze on the head or he ain't gonna last the pace."

Richard and Mandy seemed to becoming closer still.

"How does he do it?" Charlie asked himself, "he's pulled quite a piece and me and Ed couldn't even manage a couple of right dogs. I must make a note of his style for next time."

Edward became much more sensible as the soft drinks diluted the alcohol in his system. Jane, Edward and Charlie stood in a corner; the others were otherwise engaged.

"You seem a bit quiet," Charlie said to Jane, "is everything okay?"

Jane didn't reply. In fact she appeared close to tears.

"What's the matter mate," said Charlie softly.

"It won't go no further," Ed added gently.

"It's Rob" Jane began.

"What about him?" asked Charlie.

"Well," said Jane, tearfully, "since you've been away me and Rob got quite close. We were sort of seeing each other. Well, anyway, I wanted to finish it but he said that if I knocked him on the head he might say that I was involved with the stealing."

"He said that?" queried Charlie.

"Well, yeah, he definitely implied it."

"Look don't worry," said Ed "we're just going to the gents' then we'll talk."

"What do we do?" asked Charlie, as they stood in the toilet.

"He's a shit." said Edward, "if he was forcing her to go out with him when she didn't want to, that's like rape, ain't it?"

"I suppose so," said Charlie.

"The little shit grassed you as well, ain't it?"

"Yeah," answered Charlie.

"I vote that we cane the little bastard."

They talked in the toilets for about twenty minutes and, then, went to find Jane. Soon, Jane agreed.

She walked to the public phone and dialled Rob's number. She spoke for a short time, and then returned to Charlie and Edward.

"I'm meeting him at the park in ten minutes," said Jane.

Charlie, Jane and Edward bade farewell to their pals and left the pub.

When they reached the park Jane approached Rob who had already arrived. Rob didn't see Charlie and Edward until Edward grabbed him.

"We want a little chat," snarled Edward, gripping Rob by the shoulders.

Rob looked petrified.

Charlie walked towards the snivelling wreck - nothing was said.

The first punch broke Rob's nose. It was dark, but plenty of blood was visible. Rob would have fallen but Edward wasn't going to let him. Charlie had an open target; he wasn't going to waste an opportunity like this. Punch followed punch until Rob's skinny body went limp. Edward released his iron grip and Rob collapsed. Charlie, still not satisfied, rained savage kicks on the defenceless lad. All he wanted was to inflict pain - stuff the consequences.

"Don't fuck about with Jane again or, I swear, I'll fucking kill you." he yelled, almost hysterically.

Rob groaned but nothing else.

Jane, Edward and Charlie left the bloodied figure on the grass. They all appeared calm as they trudged the path homewards. No words were spoken.

114

Chapter 11

The light shining through the gap in the orange curtains stirred Charlie from his slumber the following morning.

"My bloody head" he moaned, "it feels like it's going to explode. Still, at least I'm free. I ain't looking at a barred window first thing."

He rubbed his eyes and stretched-out his arms.

"Shame that I didn't pull last night - it would have been nice to have some piece next to me this morning."

The events of the evening came flooding back.

"Shit," he murmured, "I wonder how Rob is. He looked pretty bad; I hope that he's okay."

He pictured Rob laid-out on the grass - a bloodied heap.

"Did he deserve such a beating?" he asked himself, "how can you justify that?"

He pulled himself from his bed.

"What have I become," he wondered, "a fucking savage? I mean, he deserved a little slap for grassing but what we done was well out of order. I can't even blame the bloody intrusive thoughts as I wasn't worried about anything last night."

"Could it be down to prison?" he asked himself, aloud.

"Well," he answered, "I suppose you ain't shown no mercy in prison but that ain't really an excuse."

He threw-on some clean dungarees.

"And what would Rob think if he knew you wanted to go to prison anyway? How the hell would he feel then? Yeah, he did grass but you would have made sure that you got nicked sooner or later, if he had grassed or not. And you weren't worried that it was very likely that he and the others would join you when you were nicked. Let's face it, you've treated him like a shit and then, to top it all, you knock the hell out of him."

Charlie's stomach churned.

"I feel shit. I wish I could do something to put it right. If I could do something, then I bloody would. If I get nicked for this and go to prison then that's probably the best place for me."

Charlie sloped into the kitchen. Nobody else was home so he had his own space. He sat at the table with a steaming cup of coffee.

"Do you reckon it was the booze that caused you to act like you did?" he thought.

"Don't really know," he answered himself, "must have thought about it sober."

The shrill ring of the phone interrupted his thoughts.

"Hello" said Charlie.

"Hello" said Rob.

"Fuck me," thought Charlie, wanting to be friendly but feeling that to be inappropriate.

"Just thought you'd like to know the damage," said Rob. "My nose is shattered so they've got to insert a metal plate to help me breathe. My jaw and cheekbone are fractured but they reckon they can be sorted. Oh yeah, plenty of bruises."

Charlie was desperate to apologise, beg for forgiveness, but he just couldn't get out the words.

"See ya" said Rob, not seeming to keen on a chat.

"See ya" said Charlie.

"Well" mused Charlie, wandering back into the kitchen, "I feel even guiltier now but I also feel relieved. At least Rob will be okay and it doesn't sound like he'll tell the police. Still, if I did get put away, maybe it wouldn't be so bad."

Charlie spent the next few hours thinking about Rob. To take his mind off the lad he decided to walk to the local shop and purchase some tobacco.

"I haven't had any thoughts since I got out of prison so a trip to the shop should be okay," he decided.

He left the house.

"So far, so good," he thought, as he strolled along the road, feeling more than a little anxious.

As he walked his anxiety levels gradually lowered. By the time he reached the newsagents' he was coping as well as he had hoped.

He walked into the shop - fairly confident.

"Half an ounce of Golden Virginia, please," he said to the member of staff.

"Here you are," said the old lady, handing Charlie the goods.

Charlie's heart was pumping; his anxiety levels were the highest since he had left prison.

"Oh shit," he panicked, "did I hit her?"

The image of striking the elderly woman passed through his mind. He could see her standing in front of him, unharmed, but he couldn't remove the image. It seemed so real, so frightening, so believable.

"Calm down" he urged himself, "just take the tobacco, carefully, and leave. When you pick up the tobacco be very careful that your hand doesn't knock into the old woman."

Charlie, hand shaking, took his purchase and left. As he walked along the road towards home he couldn't shake the image of him hitting the elderly shop assistant.

"Did you hit her?" he asked himself.

"No," he answered, "she was fine - I looked at her."

"What if she collapsed after you had left the shop" he pressured himself.

He became more and more anxious.

"What if she is lying behind the counter and it's all down to you?"

Charlie could take no more.

"I'll have to go and check" he decided.

He turned and retraced his steps, back to the newsagents'. As he headed back towards the shop he began to feel slightly better, he wasn't sure why. Maybe, he assumed, that soon he would no longer be as worried as he was now. He went in and purchased a box of matches. The elderly lady was fine; she even served him with a smile.

Charlie left the shop, for the second time, much happier.

"If I'd have hit her she would definitely have remembered me. She certainly wouldn't have smiled at me. That's the end of that worry. Thank Heavens."

The days passed. Charlie, often, stayed at home.

"I'm worried about getting a worry," he thought to himself.

A few days later, Charlie, feeling brave, decided to visit an indoor shopping centre with his sister, Lucy. The centre was busy, very busy. People were rushing around; they all seemed to know exactly what they were doing and what they wanted.

"Shit," panicked Charlie, "this is a bloody nightmare. I must stay in control. If I lose it that'll be it."

When Charlie saw an old lady he took evasive action.

"If I can't reach her then I won't be able to hit her," he thought, "and if I grip one hand with the other or fold my arms and grip the skin under my armpits, again, I won't hit her."

"Hang-on, Charlie," said Lucy, "I just want to look at the dresses in this shop window."

"Okay," Charlie replied and turned to look at the dresses.

Having turned, Charlie found himself next to an elderly couple.

"Did I push her or harm her?" he asked himself.

He turned to face the elderly couple.

"Bloody hell, I hope that I didn't do anything bad" he thought.

Charlie's heart thrashed against his chest, his vision became blurred, his mouth became dry and his arms and legs were shaking and unsteady.

As Charlie watched the old woman it was obvious that she was fine; or if she did have any health problems they hadn't been caused by him.

"She's fine," he told himself, "don't worry."

Reluctantly, Charlie continued to look at a purple, long-sleeved dress.

"There's no old women within reach, so keep calm," he kept telling himself.

"You okay, Charlie," asked Lucy, breaking his concentration.

"Yeah, okay," he replied "just a bit tired."

"What else could he say," he reasoned, "I can hardly tell her that I'm worried about hitting some old biddy. She'd think that I was joking or ready to be taken away by the men in white coats."

"Let's have a look in here," continued Lucy, heading towards another clothes shop.

"Okay," sighed Charlie.

Charlie glanced to his right.

"Oh shit," he panicked.

About two feet away was an elderly shopper - female. She struggled along, walking stick in one hand and a leather handbag in the other.

"Oh bollocks," thought Charlie, "did I try and grab her bag?"

"Don't be so bloody daft," he told himself, "look at her - she's fine."

"Yeah, but what if you made a lunge for the bag" he tormented himself, a horrible image forming in his mind.

As Charlie intently studied the old woman his anxiety levels, which had risen sharply, lowered. She didn't seem distressed or upset at all.

"She looks fine," decided Charlie, "not the victim of an attempted robbery."

When Charlie lost sight of the lady, his anxiety levels rose again. If it had been possible he would have watched her for the rest of the day.

"I'm sure she'll be fine," he assured himself, trying to steady his nerves.

Eventually, Lucy was ready to head home.

"What a trip to the shops," thought Charlie, "I spent the whole time checking no old women were near me and if I wasn't checking, it was only because I was worrying that I'd actually hit one of them."

Back home, Charlie headed straight for his bedroom- feeling despondent rather than anxious.

"I've got a headache," he told Lucy, "I'll be okay soon."

Charlie lay on his bed, thinking.

"I wonder why I have these bloody thoughts," he thought. "I remember reading a magazine article in Lewes about a lady who seemed to have several different personalities inside her mind. They were all different people and they tried to make her do awful things. An old man constantly told her to self-harm. She did have other personalities, as well, but I can't remember a lot about them or what they wanted her to do."

Charlie rolled onto his stomach still thinking about the article he had read in prison.

"The lady, finally, went to get help. She was eventually told that she had schizophrenia. I wonder if I could have the same thing."

Charlie rubbed his eyes. He felt anxious - thinking about schizophrenia didn't help his anxiety.

"I doubt I have got that," he decided, "because I ain't got loads of different personalities. I seem to have just one - me. There is a good side, or should I say normal side, and an evil side which makes me think that I have, or will, hit an old woman."

Charlie felt very confused as he lay secluded in his room.

"How can I expect someone to know what is going on in my head if I don't know myself?"

The young lad felt waves of sadness. He didn't cry but tears were not too far away.

"Why me?" he moaned. "What have I done to deserve these thoughts? Am I such a wicked person?"

It wasn't too long before anger played the major role.

"Why the fuck should I get this shit? Life is hell on earth and I don't give a monkey's fuck about anything. Who cares if I knock the shit out of some old biddy?"

His thoughts came to a halt. He knew that he had lied. He would rather do anything than harm an old lady.

"Charlie," he heard his sister's voice, "do you fancy a cup of coffee?"

"No point lying here," he reasoned, "got to try and live a little."

"Just coming" he shouted.

It was the following morning when the ringing of the phone disturbed Charlie's sleep. It took a great deal of effort for him to drag himself from the comfort of his bed.

"Hello" he mumbled, still half-asleep.

"Alright Chaz," he recognised Edward's gruff voice, "I want to get some new trainers, do ya fancy coming along?"

"Em… no thanks mate," Charlie remembered his last trip to the shops, "I've got a migraine."

"Okay mate," said Edward, "no problem."

"Funny how these thoughts dictate your life," thought Charlie, replacing the phone, "if I wasn't always worrying about old women I would definitely have gone with Ed."

Charlie, with little else to do, decided to watch the television. All he could find to take his mind away from elderly ladies being harmed was a cookery programme.

"Great," he thought, "but I suppose there ain't nothing else to do."

Charlie, bored beyond belief, had been sitting in the same position for about an hour. He felt a slight ache in his shoulder so he stretched-out his arm.

"Oh hell" he panicked, "was there an old woman there? Did I hit her?"

"Don't be stupid" he tried to reassure himself, "there wasn't anyone there. Certainly not an old woman. Lucy and Hazel are out so there is nobody in the house at all."

"What if an old woman had wandered into the house without me knowing and when I stretched-out I whacked her?"

"What are the chances of that? Ten million to one." he told himself, wanting to be convinced.

"You never know, it could have happened."

"So, where is this old dear now" he tried to rationalise with himself.

"She could have staggered off for help," he answered his own question.

Charlie's heart raced. He was panicking.

After a while he did manage to regain some sort of control. Nevertheless it wasn't long before a similar occurrence. More panicking. He had to do something.

"I know," he muttered, "if I propped a video cassette against the closed door then I could always tell if somebody had been in the room. If someone came in the cassette would fall over. And the good thing about it - it would be impossible to replace the cassette and get out of the room. I can't see some old dear climbing out the window. So you see, if the cassette is against the door, then nobody has been in. That is the only way, I can think of, to be sure that I ain't hit some old bird."

Charlie was happy - for the time being, anyway.

As time passed video cassettes appeared at various doors in the house.

"Not another one," said Edward, one evening, smiling.

A lot of Charlie's pals found the cassettes quite funny - none of them knew the reason why they were by the doors and not near the video recorder.

Hazel, on the other hand, found the situation a little concerning. Older and wiser, perhaps.

One afternoon, when they were alone, Hazel decided she should ask some questions.

"Is everything okay, Charlie? You seem to be acting.... well.... strangely."

"Well," replied Charlie, "I er do seem to be very anxious."

"What else can I say," thought Charlie. "I certainly ain't gonna tell her the whole truth and I don't want to give her a load of crap."

"Do you think, perhaps, that you should see someone? The doctor, maybe?" suggested his mother.

"Yes, okay," Charlie was desperate, any hope preferable to no hope.

Charlie visited Dr. Woods the following day.

"So, what can I do for you?" enquired the doctor.

"Well" stuttered Charlie, "I seem to be experiencing unwanted thoughts."

"What exactly do you mean?" asked the medic.

"I keep thinking that I've hit someone or worrying that I might," Charlie couldn't find adequate words.

The doctor looked puzzled.

"Do you feel a psychiatrist might be able to help?" he asked gently.

"Yes, I suppose so," answered Charlie.

"That's good" Charlie thought, "at least I've got the right man for the job."

"Right then," said Dr. Woods, "I'll refer you to a Dr. King. He's a lovely man. You'll be notified of an appointment as soon as possible."

Details of a meeting with Dr. King arrived by post within the week.

"Bloody hell" thought Charlie, reading the letter, "that was quick. Maybe, they think I'm dangerous or something."

Charlie stared at Dr. King across the large oak desk. The well-furnished consulting room suited the distinguished looking gentleman.

"He looks exactly as I would have imagined," thought Charlie, "slightly plump, well dressed, very educated, grey hair, pleasant face, probably about fifty-five."

"So, how exactly would you describe your problem?" began Dr. King.

"Well, em...." Charlie hesitated.

"You find it difficult to discuss?"

"I, em..... have these unwanted thoughts coming into my head. They bother me a lot."

"You've not been out of prison very long" Dr. King redirected the conversation.

"That's right," answered Charlie.

"So these intrusive thoughts - what exactly do they involve?"

"I keep thinking that I've hit someone. I never actually have but I'm always worrying about it," said Charlie.

"I just can't tell him the people I worry about are all old," thought Charlie, "he'll think I'm a fucking animal."

"How long were you in prison?" Dr. King, again, changed the line of questioning.

"I got six months for burglaries and thefts."

"Would you say the thoughts affected your daily living?" asked Dr. King.

"Yeah, they dictate most things I do."

"How would you feel about some time in Brookwood?" enquired Dr. King.

"Brookwood?" said Charlie.

"The psychiatric hospital" answered Dr. King.

"If that's what you reckon," replied Charlie.

"I suppose Brookwood could be the answer," thought Charlie, "anything has got to be worth a try."

"Right," concluded Dr. King, I will instruct my secretary to notify you the instant a bed becomes available. Hopefully, that won't be longer than a week."

A day later Charlie was watching Children's Television when the phone relieved his boredom.

"Hello, is that Mr. Lloyd?"

"Yeah," replied Charlie.

"It's Dr. King's secretary - there is a bed available at Brookwood, so would you try and be there before eleven in the morning."

"Thank-you, I will," replied Charlie.

Early the next morning Hazel drove Charlie to the hospital.

"I feel a bit sick," thought Charlie, as the car sped along, "I would even go as far to say that I'm shitting myself."

Charlie looked at his mother in the driver's seat. She smiled - nothing was said.

"I wonder if they'll know what's wrong with me?" he thought, "will they have a cure? I wonder what the other patients will be like? This place could be much worse than prison?"

"We're here," said Hazel, pointing ahead, "look."

"Oh well" thought Charlie, "all questions will be answered - very soon."

Chapter 12

The car pulled into the hospital. Charlie took great note of his surroundings. Hazel concentrated on driving.

"The gardens look really nice," thought Charlie, "so beautiful and well cared for. I can imagine sitting outside and relaxing - should do me a lot of good."

Charlie turned his gaze to the old-fashioned brick buildings.

"Don't like the look of them much," he decided, "I can imagine what has happened in them over the years. I bet loads of people have suffered - beatings, self-harm, suicide and God knows what else."

Charlie tried to ignore his first impressions of Brookwood hospital.

"As soon as I'm better I'll never have to come to a place like this again."

Charlie bid farewell to his mother at the hospital's entrance.

"Don't want her to watch me go in here," he decided. "It'll be bad enough without anyone knowing what goes on."

After filling in several forms Charlie was shown to a bed in the large, but crowded male dormitory.

"Don't like the look of this at all," he decided. "The beds are so close together. Knowing my luck I'll get a complete loon in the next bed."

Charlie unpacked his belongings and sat on his bed.

"So, what the hell do I do now?" he thought, "Do I just sit here and wait?"

Fifteen minutes had passed before a nurse peeped into the room.

"Mr Lloyd?" he asked.

Charlie nodded.

"You'll see the duty psychiatrist at six tonight. The other patients are in the smokers' room. You might like to join them."

"Yeah, I will," answered Charlie.

Charlie, without too much difficulty, found the smokers' room.

"Bloody hell" he thought, slumping down in a tatty chair as far away from everyone as he could get, "this is a horrible place. This room is so depressing. The furniture is old and in shit condition.

Nobody is talking and they all look like their best mate has just died. Not to mention the floor has more dirt on it than carpet."

There were four other residents in the room. An elderly gentleman, bespectacled with receding grey hair, who stared at the floor. His eyes were fixed on the same spot and they didn't move. He hadn't even looked-up when Charlie had walked in.

"Don't know what to make of him," thought Charlie, "seems to be in a world of his own. I ain't even sure if he knows I've come into the room. Maybe he doesn't realise that anybody else is here."

Opposite the old man was an elderly woman. She was short, painfully thin with a long face and curly grey hair. Saliva dripped from her mouth as she rocked gently in her chair.

"Blimey," thought Charlie, "and I thought I was bad. God knows what's wrong with her but she ain't in a good way. I heard a while ago that a lot of mentally ill people rock themselves. I think they do it to comfort themselves."

On the next chair was another old lady. Short and fat, she chain smoked. Before putting-out one cigarette she would use it to light the next. She looked depressed but she did seem to know the day of the week.

"Shit," thought Charlie, "two old women. I hope that I can handle this. The thoughts ain't that bad at the moment but if they do get worse while I'm in here I could be in trouble."

The last resident was a tall, skinny male, probably a year or two older than Charlie.

"I have never seen anyone look so sad" decided Charlie, "what the hell could have happened in someone's life to make them that gutted? He looks so lost, so empty, but not angry. I've seen some desperate people in prison who cut themselves but never have I seen an expression of such deep sadness."

Charlie rolled a cigarette. Feeling uncomfortable with the hanging silence he tried to think of something to say.

"What you here for, mate," he asked, looking at the skinny young man.

"Probably not the best line," he decided, "but it ain't the best situation that I've ever been in."

The young man slowly stood up. He was probably a touch over six foot. He said nothing but walked towards Charlie.

"Bloody hell" thought Charlie, "I think that he's gonna start something. This place is worse than Feltham."

Charlie climbed to his feet.

"I know that he looks sad" he thought, "a sadness I ain't never seen but I can't let him take the piss."

The young patient walked over to Charlie and...... hugged him.

"Oh God" panicked Charlie, "I hope he doesn't think that I'm dancing at the other end of the ballroom. What do I do? Hit him? Hug him? I ain't got a clue."

"It's alright love," said the chain-smoking old lady, "he does that to everyone. It's just his way of being friendly."

At just after six o'clock Charlie kept his appointment with the psychiatrist. The doctor was foreign and his command of the native tongue was severely restricted. The consultation didn't take long.

"I didn't get very far with him" thought Charlie, leaving the room, "it would have helped if we could have understood each other. Even then, I ain't sure that I would have told him everything as I'd feel a complete shit."

The next morning Charlie was alone in the smokers' room with the tall, skinny, young man."

"The same expression," thought Charlie, looking at the patient's face, "more sorrow than a thousand tears."

Charlie took a roll-up from behind his ear and lit it. The room filled with fumes. Charlie didn't want to sit in silence so he attempted to break the ice.

"Hello again" he began, "you never did tell me your name."

"It's Adrian" the voice held a sad note.

"Oh right, how long have you been here?"

"Quite some time."

"I'll see you soon" said Charlie, realising that a long conversation would be too much for Adrian.

Charlie left the room and headed for the dormitory.

"He would probably be a nice bloke if he wasn't so ill" thought Charlie, "I wonder what is wrong with him. He seems like he wants to be friendly but, for some reason, he can't."

Charlie walked down the corridor towards the dormitory. He passed an old lady running along with no trousers.

"Did I hit her," he panicked, "is that why she's running?"

"Don't be stupid" he told himself, "she was running before she passed you. Probably something to do with not wearing any trousers."

"But you still could have hit her."

"I didn't. I fucking didn't."

Charlie, very anxious, completed the trip to his dormitory. He sat on his bed, head in hands.

"Calm down" he told himself, "you did nothing wrong."

Time was a great healer. The anxiety eased - replaced by regret - replaced by sadness.

Charlie lay on his bed.

"I am an unlucky bastard with these fucking intrusions," he thought, "but now that I've been in here I know that there are a lot of people worse than me."

As the worries passed with the hours, Adrian and Charlie grew fairly close. It was a strange sort of friendship.

One afternoon Charlie and Adrian wandered into the male dormitory on another ward. Unless you were a patient on that ward the dormitories were strictly out of bounds.

"It's okay Aide," encouraged Charlie, "let's just have a nose - we ain't doing nothing wrong."

Adrian would have jumped off a cliff if Charlie thought it was a good idea.

"Alright then" Adrian replied.

On one of the beds, in the dormitory, was a male patient, obviously in an intense state of depression.

"They've just taken-away my pills," he said, without giving Charlie or Adrian a glance.

"Why?" asked Charlie.

"I was going to kill myself. I'm forty-five next week and I'm not going to see that birthday."

"Bloody hell" thought Charlie, "this bloke is in a right state. I'll try and make him laugh."

"I always thought it would be better to jump from a high window," said Charlie, "all gets sorted a lot quicker."

The man on the bed didn't appear to have heard. Probably best if he hadn't.

"Why the hell did I say that," thought Charlie, "how can you make a joke out of somebody trying to kill himself? Not really a laughing matter is it?"

Charlie glanced at Adrian who obviously didn't appreciate the joke either.

"What's going-on in here?" shouted a senior male nurse.

"Where the hell did he appear from?" thought Charlie.

Charlie turned and faced the nurse.

"Nothing" he mumbled.

"You shouldn't be here. Get back to your own dormitory." raged the nurse.

"Okay, we're going," said Charlie, "come-on, Aide."

Later in the week the grim hospital welcomed a new arrival. Jenny, a nineteen-year-old, buxom redhead had only just qualified to nurse patients with mental health needs.

Charlie chatted with Jenny much of the time. It was a rainy afternoon and Jenny and Charlie were playing pool in the games room. Jenny was having a moan about her boyfriend.

"He's always in the pub" she said.

"How long have you been together?" asked Charlie.

"About eighteen months. We've lived together for about five. I'm definitely going to chuck him out. I really would like to meet somebody else."

"She wasn't hinting, was she?" thought Charlie, "no, what would a bird like that want with a nutcase like me?"

Charlie played his next shot.

"Anyway," he thought, "there are reasons why I wouldn't go with the bird. Firstly, my unwanted thoughts are getting worse and worse so I have to get them sorted and, also, she has got a bloke and it ain't very nice to nick another bloke's bird whatever she says about him."

A day later, but not a day nearer sanity, it was feeding time at the zoo. Charlie, having forced down some of the muck, left the dining area. He passed an old lady, propped against the wall.

Charlie returned to his dormitory, panicking.

"You didn't hit that old dear," he told himself.

"You might have," the doubt was installed.

It took Charlie a while to calm himself.

"I've got to do something," he thought, "so I will get out of here on weekend leave and do a burglary. I will make sure that I get nicked and then I will be sent to Lewes. If they offer me bail I'll refuse. I know they won't put me back in this loony bin because I'm only here as a voluntary patient. I must admit I'll miss Jenny but I'm not enjoying life here because of the bloody thoughts. And I just can't bring myself to discuss the thoughts with anyone; I'd just feel too much of an animal."

Charlie sorted-out his weekend leave - all he had to do, now, was wait for Friday.

"One more day," he thought, lying on his bed, "I can't wait. Out of this hole and back to prison. I prefer it in prison and, mainly, I won't have to worry about unwanted thoughts."

Friday, as always, arrived on time. Charlie's mother arrived at the hospital to collect her son.

"See you on Monday, Jenny," said Charlie, as he packed his few belongings.

"See you on Monday, Aide," shouted Charlie, as he walked-out the hospital.

"I'll be fucked if I ever set foot in a place like this again," he thought to himself, as he climbed into the car, "what a depressing shit-hole."

Hazel made every possible effort to strike-up conversation, in the car, on the journey home.

"Have they told you what's wrong?" she asked.

"I don't think they're certain" Charlie replied with a shrug.

"Have they told you how best to deal with the condition?" Hazel asked.

"Not yet," Charlie answered, avoiding any eye contact with his mother.

"And they're not going to get a chance to help me," thought Charlie, "because I'd rather cure myself by going to prison than go back to that shit-hole."

It didn't seem that long until they arrived home. Once inside, Charlie began to prepare two cups of coffee - a milky cup for his mother and a strong cup for himself.

"So how are you feeling at the moment?" asked Hazel.

"Oh fine," he lied.

"Well, that's good," answered Hazel.

"Now, it's totally up to you but I have arranged to go out, tonight, with Joan but, if you don't want to be on your own, I can cancel. That won't be a problem."

"No, don't be silly," he answered, "I'll be fine on my own. I even feel quite relaxed."

Charlie couldn't bring himself to look at his mother.

"I feel bloody awful" he thought, "I just want to get rid of her so that I can get myself sorted. I'll lie, cheat do anything just so long as I can get away from these bloody thoughts. I'll deceive my own mother if it means getting away from these fucking intrusions."

His mother showered, threw on some clothes and left the house in a hurry.

"Bye," she called, closing the door.

The car's engine purred away from the property.

"Good" thought Charlie, "that's her gone. Lucy is at her boyfriend's so I should be okay."

Charlie watched television, drank coffee, paced the corridors ….. he just couldn't settle.

Much later, he took his screwdriver from under the bed, hid it in his jacket and headed into the darkness.

"Well, I ain't gonna be back here tonight," he reasoned, "I'll make sure, one way or another, the police make an arrest."

Charlie walked far. He passed many houses, large and small.

"No chance," he said to himself, "definitely not my style. Might frighten some old dear into her grave."

Many cars were parked along the road.

"Not serious enough," decided Charlie, "doubt the Old Bill would even turn up for a car. It needs to be something a bit bigger."

Charlie had walked for miles when he reached a clubhouse. Until now, he had never thought of breaking-in."

"Why not," he decided, "this is as good a place as any."

He walked cautiously into the private grounds, looking about.

"Must make sure there ain't no security guard who's gonna jump out and beat the crap out of me."

He reached the cluster of buildings that made up the clubhouse. Another quick check and he clambered, quite easily, onto a flat roof. It was easy to reach a window. He removed the slats of the louvred window - no problems so far. The jump was about twelve feet.

"Nobody about," he thought, "let's do it."

He landed, knees bent, on the carpeted floor. The bar was only feet away from him. Four or five fruit machines were within spitting distance. "Fuck me," thought Charlie, "I could make a fortune."

The alarm screeched - Charlie had only been in the room a matter of seconds.

"I wouldn't have had time to nick much," thought Charlie, "if that's what I was after."

Charlie didn't panic. He was remarkably composed as he pulled himself onto the window ledge.

"Couldn't care if the police turn up. I want to get nicked anyway."

Charlie stepped on to the flat roof, hesitated, then jumped to the reddish gravel below. He walked, calmly, away from the clubhouse. He had no intention of leaving the area. He plodded fifty yards along the road, until he came across a wooden bench.

"Might as well sit here," he decided, it's as good a place as any. Hope the pricks hurry up and get here."

He heard the sirens long before he saw the cars. A marked car, with two officers, pulled-up alongside Charlie.

"Hello Charlie," said one officer, the big nose looked familiar, "what have you been doing?"

"Nothing," replied Charlie.

The two officers exchanged glances.

"Don't want to confess straight-away," decided Charlie, "or they'll know I want to go to prison and then they might ask some awkward questions."

"Well, somebody has just tried to burgle the sports club," said Strawberry Nose. "Then we find you, a person known to us, not a hundred yards away. How do you explain that?"

"Can't really, guv," answered Charlie. "Just taking a rest."

Charlie studied the ground.

"Hurry up and arrest me you thick shit," he thought, "ain't it obvious, even to you?"

"Could you show me the soles of your trainers?" asked Strawberry Nose.

Charlie removed his trainers and gave them to the officer.

"You've got red dust on your shoes," said Strawberry Nose. "I'm arresting you for attempted burglary. You do not have to say anything but what you do say can and will be used as evidence against you in a court of law....."

"About time," thought Charlie. "He'll be a sergeant by the time he's finished with me."

Charlie lay on the wooden bench in his cell at the police station covered by a dirty, woollen blanket. He had been charged with attempted burglary and bail had been withheld. He would go before the magistrates' in the morning - he would not apply for bail. Short of a natural disaster, Charlie would be in Lewes prison the following night.

"I feel gutted for Hazel," thought Charlie. She's tried to help but she doesn't know what the thoughts can do. Some of my mates will be shocked, but they could never understand what it's like for me trying to live a normal life. I can't tell them either."

Charlie rolled over and snuggled into the blood-stained blanket and drifted into sleep.

Chapter 13

The following morning Charlie was remanded for seven days to Lewes jail. He was soon on the same wing and landing. He recognised a few familiar faces, but largely the personnel had altered. He was sharing a cell with Dominic, a small, shy lad of seventeen who definitely wasn't suited to prison. Dominic seemed to have a sharp brain and the cell-mates enjoyed many long discussions.

"I got remanded for stealing a car," Dominic told Charlie, "I would never have normally done anything like that but my mate persuaded me. He's over on the adult wing. I had so much respect for him I would have done almost anything he asked. I guess that I just wanted to be like him. He's so outgoing and popular whereas I've only got one mate and that's him."

It was a Friday afternoon. Dominic and Charlie had just finished their lunch. It was the usual - tasteless fish and chips.

"That was horrible," moaned Dominic.

"Oh, you soon get used to the muck," replied Charlie, rubbing his stomach.

"I could never get used to anything in a place like this," continued Dominic, "it really has taught me a lesson. I will never steal again and I don't care who asks me to."

"You will get used to being here," answered Charlie, "the first few weeks are always the worst. When you get into a routine the days fly past."

"Do you want a fag?" asked Dominic.

"Yeah lovely," answered Charlie.

"I don't think I can get used to this place," Dominic went on, "I couldn't even survive school. I got bullied most of the time because I was the smallest and weakest."

"Honestly mate," said Charlie, "the time will go quite quickly. If you keep yourself to yourself, you can avoid a lot of trouble."

A key in the lock. The door was about to be opened.

"Lloyd, visit," announced the warden.

"Fuck, shit," panicked Charlie, "what the hell am I going to do now? I can't go out on a visit - think of all those old women. I'll be worried for months if I have to go out there and face all those old dears. These bloody thoughts - they fuck everything."

Charlie looked at Dominic then turned his gaze back to the warden.

"I'm sorry guv, but I don't want the visit," Charlie said.

"What? You don't know who it is 'til you get out there," replied the officer, sounding surprised, "are you quite sure?"

"Yeah, I am" said Charlie, "thanks guv."

The warden gave a shrug and closed the door.

"Bloody thoughts," thought Charlie, "for most people that's the beauty of being on remand - you don't have to send a visiting order so it's usually a nice surprise when you get out into the visiting room. I really would love to know who's come to see me but the fear of all those old women freaks me out."

A few days later Charlie was sitting in reception chatting to another young offender.

"Got remanded again," said Charlie, "for another week."

"Me in all," replied Andy, "been to Reigate."

"I've been to Dorking - go every week and every week it's the same - seven days further remand. Still, I must admit I do quite like it because it gets you out of this dump for a day. Did you try for bail today?"

"No mate," answered Andy, "I'll be in here now until I'm sentenced."

"What you looking at?" asked Charlie.

"I'll have to go to Guildford Crown - probably get three years," answered Andy.

"What did you do?" questioned Charlie

"Held-up a post office with a water pistol" said Andy.

"Oh."

A day after the usual court appearance and Charlie was on the ones' landing trying to choose a good book from the small selection the wardens called a library.

"Got to get something good," mused Charlie, "as reading really helps pass the time when you're banged-up."

Charlie picked up a true crime story.

"This looks okay," he thought, "quite a thick book - should take me a while to read."

Then he chose a love story.

"Nice to dream," he thought, studying the front of the book.

"What the hell did you choose that shit for?" laughed Colin, one of Charlie's mates.

"A bit of romance and you might not have ended-up in here," replied Charlie, grinning.

"Love 'em and leave 'em" said Colin, "ain't worth getting all soppy over some tart. If I hadn't been with a bird I wouldn't be here now."

"What do you mean?" asked Charlie

. "Well, some geezer shagged my bird so I stabbed him," replied Colin, "now I'm looking at six years. He was only in hospital a few weeks."

"Wouldn't want to fuck with this bloke," decided Charlie, "he's tall, well-built and I reckon he must have some temper. And, obviously, he ain't worried about using a blade. Rather have him as a mate than an enemy."

"Blood Red Kisses For Sarah," said Colin, looking at Charlie's book, "is it a bit….. well….. you know?"

"'Fraid not mate," answered Charlie, "it's just a couple who fall in love against all the odds."

"Rather have a cum mag," said Colin. "See you a bit later."

Charlie left the library and began the climb to the fours. He strolled along the top landing, and then turned into his cell.

"Give me your fucking fags, Taylor," snarled Chris Banks, slapping Charlie's terrified cellmate.

"Shit," thought Charlie, "Dom is shitting himself. Banks looks ready to go. I've got to do something and talking ain't the answer."

Charlie strode across the room. Two large strides and Banks was within reach.

"Leave him alone, you slag," snarled Charlie, as he struck with his right onto the back of Banks' head.

Banks didn't have time to turn-around. He stumbled onto the bed as the second punch connected. Then, once more, Charlie's fist hit the back of Banks' head. Charlie stepped back - point proven. He watched intently as Banks dragged himself from the bed and went to the door.

"Don't try taxing again or it will be bad," said Charlie, quite softly - no need to shout.

"Thanks," stammered Dominic, looking close to tears, "I just didn't know what to do."

"No problem" answered Charlie, feeling close to collapse, "what are mates for?"

"Do you think Banks and his mates will get us?" asked Dominic, shaking noticeably.

"I ain't sure," answered Charlie, "I doubt it."

Charlie looked at Dominic.

"Don't want him to start panicking," he thought, "but I reckon we'll be in trouble. Banks has got a lot of mates in here and he won't let anyone think that he's gone soft. We could be in for a right hiding."

At the end of each day Charlie felt a sense of relief that he had survived.

"In a way," he decided, "I'd rather they'd just get it over with. I'm sure that I'm due a slap and I spend all my time worrying about what's gonna happen. If they'd just knock the crap out of me I could get on with each day without looking over my shoulder."

It was a grim, overcast Tuesday and Dominic and Charlie were banged-up. Charlie was reading a romantic novel and Dominic was writing a romantic letter to an ex-girlfriend.

"Slop-out," bellowed an officer.

Doors started opening as the wardens paced the landing.

Charlie and Dominic stood chatting.

"Taylor, visit," said Mr. Scott, the duty officer.

"It'll be my sister, Diane," Dominic said to Charlie.

Dominic followed Scottie along the landing.

Charlie stood alone.

"I need a piss," he decided, "better to go now than have to use that bloody chamber-pot later."

Charlie left the recess and headed towards his cell. He entered the room. He felt acute pain as the powerful blow landed on the back of his bald head. The floor came to meet him. He covered his head with his hands and lay still.

"What the fuck are they going to do to me," he tried to think clearly, "this could be it. The end."

His body jolted. The kicking was savage. It didn't seem to end. Finally, it did.

"They must have gone," Charlie thought, "I reckon it'll be okay to try and lift my head."

His head ached like mad, but he was alone.

"My body feels like I've been hit by a car," he moaned, "those bastards weren't fucking about. Oh, what I'd give for a tasty little nurse and some loving care. No chance."

Charlie rubbed his chest.

"Shit," he panicked, "I'm soaking wet. Blood? Did the bastards stab me?"

He strained his sore neck to see the extent of the damage. How much blood and where it was all coming from.

"I can't see any blood" he thought, "but I am definitely soaked."

He glanced around the cell. Suddenly he realised.

"Dirty scum. Fucking bastards. They've only emptied Dom's pisspot over me."

He could smell the stale urine on his clothes and see the empty chamber pot on the floor.

"I've got to have a shower and get changed" he thought, "my body feels fucked but I must wash. Those shits, not happy with beating the crap out of me, have made me feel a right dirty bastard."

Charlie, physically sore and mentally degraded, looked round the room for some spare clothes. He found a tracksuit belonging to Dominic. He struggled to the shower. He washed vigorously, ignoring the pain from his bruised body.

"How humiliating" he thought, "I feel a right shit. I think I'd have rather been stabbed."

Charlie had been in the shower for twenty minutes.

"Better hurry," he thought, "the screws will want us to bang-up soon. I look bloody clean but I can still smell piss. I'm covered in red marks - I'm going to have some bruises tomorrow. I hope nothing is broken."

Charlie, with the smell of urine burning in his nostrils, hobbled back to his cell.

"Alright Dom," he said, "Did you have a good visit? Have I got news for you."

Charlie told Dominic what he had missed while he was chatting to his sister. Owing to his change of clothes he had little choice but to inform Dominic why the chamber pot was empty.

"Do you reckon they'll be after me now?" asked Dominic, trembling visibly.

"I doubt it," said Charlie, "they've proved they ain't to be messed with - hopefully they'll leave it alone."

"I feel sick," said Dominic, sitting on the bed.

"Don't worry," offered Charlie, mopping the floor. "I'm sure the matter is closed as far as they're concerned."

"You don't want to do anything to them, do you?" asked Dominic.

"I won't," said Charlie, "I don't need any more grief."

Charlie finished cleaning the floor and sat on his bed - aching.

"I really want to get even with Banks," he thought, "but he's got loads of mates and I ain't got many people who would back me. And, if possible, I don't want to get Dominic involved in any trouble."

It was evening slop-out. Dominic, Charlie and Colin stood, chatting, on the landing.

"Did you have a good visit," Colin asked Dominic.

"Yeah, really nice," said Dominic, "but my whole family are gutted about where I am."

"That's very normal," said Charlie, "my mum hates me being in a place like this."

"Are you okay, Charlie," asked Colin, tactfully not mentioning anything about chamber pots.

"I'll live," said Charlie, "there's always somebody worse off than me."

"Lock - up, please, Mr. Hartford. Immediately. Get them behind their doors." the senior officer's command could be heard at each end of the landing.

Mr. Hartford, the senior officer and two wardens from the third landing acted - speed being of the essence. Every inmate was banged-up….. within minutes.

"What's going on?" asked Dominic, sounding more than a little concerned.

"Oh, nothing for us to worry about," replied Charlie, "something's kicked-off and they want everyone out of the way."

"What do you reckon it is?" Dominic sounded curious.

"Don't know, but the flap's open so I should be able to see," Charlie said, indicating the flap on the door which the officers had forgotten to close.

Charlie walked to the door and peered through the flap.

"All the doors are shut and the screws are standing around a cell halfway along the landing, on the other side," said Charlie.

"Come on Adams," the senior officer shouted through the door, "this ain't gonna solve anything."

"It's Adams' cell," said Charlie to Dominic, "the nutter must have barricaded himself in."

"Who is Adams?" asked Dominic.

"Oh, you would have seen him," answered Charlie, "very tall, dark hair, looks a bit mad."

"What's he in here for?" questioned Dominic.

"Armed robbery," answered Charlie, "but I think he shot someone while he was doing it. As far as I know he's spent a bit of time in the funny farm, as well."

"Why don't the screws just unlock the door and force their way in?" asked Dominic.

"Well" said Charlie, "the two beds lengthways are the same length as the cell, so if you put them against the door it can't be opened."

"So what do they do?"

"They've got a machine which can force the door. Trouble is, when the door is forced it comes away at such a speed that the person in the cell could get badly hurt, even killed." Charlie said.

"Why haven't the screws got the machine," asked Dominic.

"I ain't sure. Something weird must be happening," answered Charlie, his head still at the flap.

140

"Adams, just move the bed so we can help you" the senior officer pleaded.

"There ain't much time, son," tried Mr. Hartford.

"That's right, Adams, quick as you can."

"I think he's letting them in," said Charlie to Dominic.

The wardens filed into the cell. Seconds later, they reappeared with Adams. The prisoner, barely able to walk, was covered in blood. His arms stretched to the front, cautiously supported by two wardens.

"What's happening?" asked Dominic.

"They've got him out. He's slashed both his wrists. Looks a right mess. That's why they didn't get the machine - not enough time. He looks really weak - he can hardly walk."

"Where's his cell-mate?" asked Dominic.

"I doubt he had one," answered Charlie, "if you're a bit of a nutter or a bit dangerous then the screws try and give you a single cell."

"Do you reckon he really wanted to die?" asked Dominic.

"Could have done," said Charlie, "he's gonna get a long time and he obviously ain't very stable."

"I hate this place," said Dominic, "but I would never kill myself. I'd be too scared."

"Not worth killing yourself" answered Charlie, "lots of things are worse than this."

"Like what?" asked Dominic.

"I ain't sure," replied Charlie "but there must be."

Charlie lay on his bed. Dominic sat at the table and started to write a letter.

"Horrible thoughts are worse than being in here," Charlie thought, staring at the window, "I suppose they could have driven me over the edge. Yes, with those thoughts, suicide wouldn't be out of the question."

Four days later and Charlie was enjoying his weekly trip to court. He stood in the dock staring intently at the presiding magistrate.

"Mr. Lloyd, you have the right to opt for trial by Judge and jury at the crown court or, if we are able, we can hear your case here. Where would you like your case to be heard?"

"I would like my case to be heard here," answered Charlie.

The magistrates considered the request with immense care. It seemed like ages before the presiding magistrate spoke.

"Due to the seriousness of the case we find it unsuitable for summary trial. You will appear before the crown court. You shall be notified of the date."

"Oh well" thought Charlie "I ain't really bothered. I was expecting to go to crown court, anyway."

Charlie didn't apply for bail. He was quite happy on his way back to Lewes. He would stay there until Guildford Crown Court was ready for him.

The following morning, after a pitiful breakfast, Charlie wandered around the landing.

"Hello mate," said Stuart, interrupting Charlie's private thoughts. "Are you going down the gym today?"

"Ain't nothing better to do," replied Charlie.

"Oh yeah," continued Stuart, "have you got any good books? I need an interesting read."

"Yeah Stu," said Charlie, "got a blinder about hitmen."

Then, it wasn't planned, it just happened.

"You fucking slag." It was only a thought, wasn't it? It was an intrusion beyond Charlie's control. He hadn't actually said it, had he?

"Shit," Charlie tried to make sense of what had happened. "I'm sure I didn't say anything but where did the idea come from?"

Charlie needed time…. and space.

"Got something to do in my cell" he said, "see you later, Stu."

Charlie hurried to his cell. Dominic was at classes. Charlie was alone.

"Fuck. Fuck. Fuck." he panicked, "what the hell is happening to me?"

He sat on the bed, stood up, and then paced the room.

"Calm down" he urged himself, "just calm down."

He sat on the bed, head in hands.

"First things first," he reasoned. "Did I call Stuart a fucking slag? Obviously, I had no reason to say that to him. I ain't sure where the words came from or why they were there.

142

The idea was in my head - I can't argue with that - but, I'm sure, I didn't say anything aloud."

Charlie regained a little of his composure.

"It is a very similar problem to the idea of hitting an old woman" he reasoned, "I can't stop myself thinking I've hit an old lady but I can stop myself acting on the thought. It must be the same - I can't stop the idea from coming into my brain but I am able to stop myself from saying anything aloud."

"What if you did call Stu a fucking slag?" his evil voice badgered him.

"No chance," the unspoken conversation continued, "I've never hit an old woman so why should I have said those words. I really believe that hitting old women and saying insulting things to people is only in my head. They are thoughts...... only thoughts."

Charlie rolled a cigarette. He was no longer shaking.

"Just to be sure," he mused, "I'll go and talk to Stu. If he's okay and doesn't start hitting me then I've got no need to worry."

Charlie left the security of his cell.

"Stu, what are you doing?" Charlie shouted along the landing.

"Not much," answered Stuart, tone friendly, "are you alright?"

"Fine," answered Charlie, "just fine."

"That settles it," thought Charlie, returning to his cell, "If I had treated Stu like a shit he'd have knocked me out. He certainly wouldn't have asked if I was okay. And he ain't the type of bloke to take something like that as a joke."

Charlie lay on his bed, hands behind his head.

"I'm sure that I didn't say anything out of order," he thought, "thing is - an intrusive thought did because me a lot of grief. Bastards. They've even got to me in here."

Chapter 14

Charlie had been in custody for nearly three months. One rainy morning the officer on duty opened the cell earlier than usual.

"You're in Guildford Crown Court this morning, Lloyd. Get your stuff together and wait at the gates."

"Are you sure, guv? I ain't been told."

"I'm definite, now get a move on."

"Shit," thought Charlie, as he hurried to the recess to have a quick wash, "I could get out today. What will happen then? How the bloody hell am I going to cope with the intrusions? I know that I need help but I certainly ain't going back to Brookwood. I might have to get myself put back in here. And what about the new problems I've been having - the speaking worries. I hope I can cope with them. I hope they don't make it too difficult to stay in prison."

There was one other inmate in the washroom.

"What you doing, Ian?" Charlie was pleased to see his mate.

"Guildford Crown this morning, mate," said Ian, "what about you?"

"Same," answered Charlie, happy to have a mate with him.

It was strange, but nice, to see the outside world on the trip to Guildford. On arrival at the court Charlie and Ian were banged-up together. The rest of the prisoners in court that day were over twenty-one; they were held in a separate cell.

"So what do you reckon will happen to you today," asked Charlie.

"Well, it's possible I could go home. I'm up for three burglaries - two non-dwellings and a house. I've done ten months in Lewes so my brief reckons I could get an intensive probation course. What about you?"

"Hoping for a fine," said Charlie, "been on remand three months so it's possible. I told my solicitor that I ain't prepared to do community service - can't be bothered with all that."

"You're mad," said Ian, "I'd do community service if they'd just let me out."

"I don't think you would if you had these bloody intrusions," thought Charlie, "I can't cope walking along the road, think how bad it would be working outside all day. How the hell would I manage if some old dear walked past?"

However much Charlie liked Ian he wasn't prepared to share his concerns.

"I feel lucky," offered Charlie, shrugging, "why do all that work when you can get away with a little fine?"

Charlie paced the cell.

"So what would you do if you got out?" Charlie asked his pal.

"I'd go to the nearest boozer and get lashed, then try my luck with any old dog available."

"Do you reckon you'll be back?"

"You know what they say," replied Ian, "you know the score you've been there before, you know the crack you're coming back. Saying that, I hope that I can go straight. If I do carry-on with crime I ain't doing any more dwellings. They just ain't worth it - a lot of time for fuck all."

The door opened.

"Lunch, lads," said the warden, handing the two prisoners a packed-lunch.

"A cheese sandwich and a couple of biscuits," said Charlie, his mouth full, "better than the muck we're used to."

It wasn't long before the door opened again.

"Whittaker, court five."

"Good luck, mate," said Charlie, as Ian followed the warden out the cell.

Charlie sat alone, stretched-out on the bench.

"What have I done to deserve this," he wondered, "I'm not a bad person and I was given every chance in life. I could have made something of myself if it wasn't for these bloody thoughts. Now I've gone down this road is there any chance that I'll be able to start again?"

The door opened, disturbing his concentration.

"Lloyd, your barrister will see you now."

Charlie followed the jailer along the corridor to a small room.

"Mr. Lloyd?"

Charlie nodded.

"I'm Mr. Groves and I shall be representing you today."

145

Charlie glanced at the young, clean-shaven lawyer of average height and slim build.

"Can't have much experience," decided Charlie, "he ain't a lot older than me."

"So Mr. Lloyd" continued the brief, apparently oblivious to his client's reservations, "what shall we ask for today?"

"Well" began Charlie, "I've been in for a while so what about a fine?"

"Doubtful, with your previous convictions. Would you consider community service?"

"No," replied Charlie, not bothering to offer an explanation.

"The court's hands are tied - you haven't given them a lot of options."

Mr. Groves stood up.

Try not to worry - we'll do our best."

Charlie was taken back to his cell. He sat on the bench and waited.

"At least I'll know soon," he thought, "will I have to cope with prison or will I have to worry about intrusions. I'm fucking stuck between a rock and a hard thing."

It wasn't long before the door swung open.

"Lloyd, court seven. Let's go, mate."

Heart in mouth, Charlie trailed behind his bulky guide up the stone steps to the courtroom.

"Whatever happens," he thought, "it doesn't really matter. I just want to know. Tonight, I could be sleeping in my own bed, maybe with some young lovely, or in some shit-hole, with a vomiting junkie."

The Prosecution gave an accurate and detailed account of the prisoner's misdemeanours. Then it was the turn of the defence.

"Go on mate," Charlie silently encouraged his 'legal eagle'.

The young barrister slowly arose, took a sip from a glass of water, cleared his throat, and then spoke.

"This geezer is meant to be fucking brilliant," thought Charlie, "he'll get me out of here; no problem."

"My client didn't burgle a house," said the young wizard.

"Right, what now?" asked Charlie, silently.

The lawyer sat down.

"They know that I didn't burgle a house," Charlie chatted to the lawyer inside his mind, "now give them a reason to let me go. Make them feel sorry for me. Get them reaching for the tissues. Tell them lies - because they, sure as hell, wouldn't believe the truth.

The lawyer didn't move.

"Come on, mucker," urged Charlie, silently, "you've studied years to get where you are - hit them with some magic."

The lawyer still didn't move. It was obvious, to all who were present, that he had finished.

Slowly, very slowly, it dawned on Charlie.

"What a wanker," Charlie thought, not knowing whether to laugh or cry, "I ain't been dealt a good hand. That little shit has probably spent the last few nights thinking about some tart; certainly not my case, anyway. I must be the most unlucky shit ever to grace these courtrooms - a disturbed mind and a fucking hopeless brief. If he is seeing some slapper...... well, I hope she gives him herpes."

The Judge cleared his throat. He stared at Charlie.

Charlie stared back. The sentence had been decided. There was nothing he could do.

"Nine months, Young Offenders' Institution. Take him down."

"That's it then" thought Charlie, "my immediate future has been decided in ten minutes and it was obvious that my solicitor didn't give a shit. I suppose he gets his money.... whatever happens. Probation or ten years - why should he care?"

Ian was waiting in the cell.

"How did you get on, Charlie?" he asked.

"Nine months. What about you?"

"Judges' Remand. I'll be sentenced in three weeks."

"Should be going back soon," said Charlie.

Eventually the warden opened the door.

"Are we going back to Lewes?" asked Charlie, fancying a change of scenery.

"Lewes?" questioned the officer.

"Yeah, we left there this morning."

"I don't know where you were this morning but everybody here will be taken to Brixton."

147

Charlie looked at Ian. Ian returned his gaze. They both looked at the officer. He was serious.

"This ain't a sick joke," decided Charlie.

"Oh fuck," he said.

Ian stayed silent…. gutted.

"What a wank," thought Charlie, "I could have handled a bit more of Lewes, but Brixton….. oh no."

The prison van pulled into the infamous jail. The grisly rumours that Charlie had heard seemed very possible….. extremely probable, in fact. Most sane convicts feared this destructive hole; this was the prison everyone wanted to avoid.

"Come back Feltham, all is forgiven" Charlie murmured to Ian.

Inside the grim building and things didn't improve. You had more chance of seeing a smiling face at a funeral. Violence simmered just, only just, below the surface.

"Anything could be taken the wrong way," thought Charlie, "a careless remark; even looking at the wrong person and there could be trouble. And trouble would be more than a bleeding nose."

Charlie, staring straight ahead, followed Ian and the other new inmates to the holding cell.

They waited in silence. Nobody wanted to speak - what if they said the wrong thing? The atmosphere was tense, very bloody tense. Without warning, or a raised voice, two inmates started fighting. They were on the opposite side of the cell to Charlie but the ferocity of the scrap could be felt by the young prisoner. Fists and feet lashed at anything within reach. Inmates, scared by the savagery, looked away. They weren't going to get involved; they certainly didn't want somebody to attack them. Others laughed and joked. Violence was a way of life for them - the strongest survived. They had seen it many times before; they weren't going to show signs of weakness.

From somewhere an alarm sounded. Then pounding feet could be heard. The wardens streamed into the holding cell, safe in their large numbers.

"Bloody hell" thought Charlie, "do they really need that many for two blokes? How many would they get for a riot?"

The two brawling men were separated and dragged from view. Cries and shouts could be heard long after they had gone.

"Watching a scrap is worse than having one," decided Charlie, "it always looks so fucking vicious when you ain't involved. Those punches and kicks looked bloody terrible but I doubt either of those geezers will have ended-up in the hospital. Probably be down the block getting a lot worse."

"If this is Brixton, then I don't like it," whispered Ian.

"I know what you mean," replied Charlie, keeping his voice low, "we've haven't even been here an hour and two shits are trying to kill each other."

Finally, taken to the wing, they were allocated a cell.

"Do you blokes want to bang-up together?" asked the warden.

"Yes please, guv," replied Ian, looking at Charlie.

Charlie nodded.

"Better the devil you know" he decided, "Ian's a nice bloke - I could get a lot fucking worse than him. Some smelly tramp who never washes or a complete nutter who ain't on the same planet."

The accommodation was grim. The cell stunk of stale urine and when Charlie touched the radiator he got more than he had bargained for - a pair of soiled underpants.

"Fuck me," moaned Charlie, removing his hand with lightening speed, "you do get some dirty shits in these places."

"I know mate," replied Ian, "just because you're treated like an animal doesn't mean you have to behave like one."

That night as Charlie lay in his bed he didn't feel at ease with himself or his new surroundings.

"Hope that I ain't here long," he thought, "just feel edgy. Ain't sure why. Ian's a smashing bloke, it's just this place. You feel that something bad, really bad, could happen at any time."

It was a while before Charlie drifted into a fitful sleep. Were the voices in his dreams or people calling from their barred windows?

Their first morning in Brixton - 'canteen'. They purchased some tobacco and trudged back to their cell. It wasn't long, perhaps only seconds, before they had company. Two fellow prisoners - black, shaven heads, gold teeth and big muscles - stood inside the cell.

Feltham flashed through Charlie's mind.

"Oh hell" he panicked.

"Do us some burn, star," demanded the larger of the two men.

149

Charlie hesitated. He was tempted to obey. He knew he mustn't.

"Can't do it, can we Chaz?" Ian wasn't about to be taxed.

"That's right," said Charlie, loyal to the point of a battering.

Ian, then Charlie, stepped forward.

"Shit," thought Charlie, "could get a bad thrashing. Got to stand by my mate. If I don't I'll lose a good pal and look a right wanker."

The slightly smaller, but very aggressive, black lad made a grab for Ian. His pal stood in the way.

"Leave it," he ordered, "these two shits ain't worth a wank. They'll keep for later."

"Anytime," snarled Ian.

"Don't push it," thought Charlie, hoping to avoid a scrap they probably wouldn't win.

One of the black lads spat on the stone floor. Then the pair turned and walked out the cell.

Charlie breathed a sigh of relief.

"Thank fuck," he thought, "we didn't get a thrashing and we've still got our smokes. Pucker. And, we didn't roll-over."

The days passed slowly.

"At least," thought Charlie, as he lay on his bed, "I ain't got any intruding thoughts. I reckon it must be this place - I'm always on the edge, worried about something, so I ain't got time for the bastard intrusions. I just hope that when I settle the intrusions don't come back."

They had been in Brixton for four days. Lunch had been served and Charlie and Ian were trying to eat as much as they could.

"I think this is meant to be liver," suggested Ian, trying to cut a slice of meat.

"Yeah, it ain't all that," replied Charlie, "I'll be glad to leave this dump behind. Everything about it is shit."

After lunch, Charlie and Ian read until the door was unlocked for slop-out. Charlie strolled to the recess with his dirty plates.

"Better to get my plates clean straightaway," he thought. "Can't stand all the dried food stuck to them."

He joined the back of the queue. It wasn't long before it was his turn. He was just about to rinse his dinner plate under the hot tap when a prisoner, tall, solid and with tattoos covering most of his face and neck, opted to ignore the queue.

"Wait your turn, mate," Charlie said.

Quick as lightening, the home-made knife, a razor melted onto a toothbrush, pressed against Charlie's throat.

"I'm here for murder," growled the prisoner, "one more ain't gonna make no difference."

"Fair enough," stammered Charlie, "I can always do my plates later."

Charlie returned to the solitude of his cell.

"Got to calm down" he told himself, "it was just one of those things. A bit of bad luck. Most of the other prisoners in the queue would have shit themselves too. He was a nutter; he'd have slashed you without a second thought. You did the best thing. Being brave could have cost you..... well, God knows."

Ian came back to the cell just before bang-up.

"I had a bit of grief," Charlie said to Ian, relating the events during slop-out.

"I reckon you did the right thing," said Ian. "He stabbed his best pal. It ain't no good being a dead hero."

"Good job I was near the bogs, weren't it?" said Charlie, "that was one scary geezer."

Charlie had been in Brixton nearly a week. One evening Ian and Charlie were both reading when the door was unlocked.

"Feltham tomorrow, Lloyd. Be ready, first thing," said the officer.

The door slammed shut.

"I ain't sorry to be leaving," said Charlie to Ian. "Gutted you ain't coming too but we always knew you would stay here 'til you went back to Guildford Crown."

"Yeah," replied Ian, "not long 'til court, anyway."

"You will keep in touch," said Charlie, "you've still got the address, ain't you?"

"I have mate, don't worry."

Charlie sat on the prison coach. Soon he, along with twenty other young prisoners, would be on route to Feltham.

Charlie took a long, last look at Brixton prison.

"What a shit-hole," he thought, "apart from Ian that place has only shit memories. I feel degraded just looking at the hole. It seems that the system take all the really bad cases and put them in here. Nutters, really violent cases……. it has them all. And the mess, the grime…… well, fucking hell. It would take me a long time to get used to all that."

At Feltham the allocation unit beckoned. All the convicted young offenders were sent here until a placement was decided. This could be at Feltham or any young offenders' institution across the country. Most short term, non-violent offenders would find themselves in open conditions.

Charlie sat in his cell…… pondering.

"Shit," he thought, "I hope that I don't get open conditions. Without being locked-up my mind and the bloody intrusive thoughts would make life a misery. I mean, after a while, I had problems in Hollesley Bay."

It was the following day. Each inmate had an appointment with the allocation officer. It wasn't long before it was Charlie's turn.

"Lloyd, isn't it?"

"That's right, guv."

"Well, we feel that……."

"Look guv" interrupted Charlie, "if I go to an open prison, I'll abscond the first chance I get."

"Right lad, closed prison for you. You'll be told later today where you are going."

"I've definitely done the best thing" thought Charlie, leaving the room, "I'd rather get my head punched-in by some mad shit than have to deal with my own fucking mind in open conditions."

Later that afternoon the inmates were watching a video.

"This is crap," whispered Charlie to the lad next to him.

A warden demanded silence.

"The following prisoners are staying here.

A-wing: Abbott, Timms , Walker and Williams.

D-wing: Davies, Lawson and Vickers.

E-wing: Anderson, Bell and Lloyd.

Right, you lot, get your gear together and follow me."

Charlie had been on Eagle Unit a couple of days.

"You're going to be cleaning the wing, Lloyd," said the officer, standing by the door, "everyone has to work."

"Wing cleaner," thought Charlie, "that should help to pass the time. Only got about six weeks to do, anyway."

One morning, as usual, Charlie was conscientiously scrubbing the shower-block floor. A tall, stockily-built black inmate brushed past to use a basin. He didn't speak, just filled one of the basins with icy water. Then he bent-over to wash his face.

Charlie didn't attempt to strike-up a conversation; just continued with his task.

A few minutes later and there was another arrival. Long-haired, white, sturdily-built and scarred arms.

Charlie felt anxious - he wasn't sure why.

The white inmate stood behind the lad washing his face. He opened his coat and pulled-out a thick piece of wood, about two feet long. He didn't utter a sound as he firmly, viciously, brought the wood down on the black prisoner's head. The black lad slumped to the stone floor, his face colliding with the basin as he fell. The attacker dropped his weapon and strolled out. Charlie gathered his cleaning equipment and followed.

It was a couple of weeks after his arrival and Charlie had adjusted to the new regime. He was in the lunch queue to collect his beef-pie.

Mason, a tall inmate with ginger hair and covered in tattoos, served a generous slice.

"That's lovely, mate," said Charlie.

"You lousy bastard" the thought 'spoke' in his head.

Charlie had no time to react. Feeling slightly sick, slightly dizzy, slightly numb, he collected the rest of his meal.

Charlie sat in his cell. He couldn't manage a mouthful of his food.

"Did I speak aloud," he panicked. "Were the words just in my head or did I actually say them?

Whatever I do, wherever I am, these bastard thoughts manage to ruin my life."

I must 'check' the worry. The only way would be to talk to Mason and see how he acts towards me."

Charlie lay on his bed, anxious and depressed. He did try to keep calm. He considered his plight.

"So what if you did call Mason a lousy bastard?"

"I just don't need the aggravation," he answered his own question.

Charlie rolled onto his front.

"These thoughts are like a twisted part of my mind," he mused, "they want to because me as much trouble and distress as possible. I'm certain that I didn't say anything out of order to Mason but I just can't convince myself. There's always that evil little part of me trying to cast doubts....... make me anxious about things I haven't done........ trying to convince me that I have said something or hit someone."

It seemed like forever but, soon enough, the doors were opened.

"Get to work," yelled the warden.

"Fuck work" thought Charlie, heading towards Mason, "I've got far more important things to do."

"Tony," said Charlie, "have you got any good books?"

"I ain't, mate," answered Mason, "sorry."

"Don't worry," answered Charlie "thanks, anyway."

Charlie turned away.

"Brilliant," he thought, "that was good enough. He wasn't unfriendly. Therefore, I can be sure I didn't say anything out of order. It was all in my head. It was a thought, nothing more, just a bastard thought."

Charlie was transformed. He strolled towards the cleaning cupboard, a happy young man. Life, for now, was magical - a first kiss, falling in love, losing your 'cherry' or, even better, confirming that an intrusion had not been acted upon.

The days passed. Worries caused by the evil little voice, inside Charlie's head, came and went. Charlie had much checking to do. Nobody seemed to have taken offence - thank God.

It was the night before Charlie's release. Charlie contemplated the prospect of freedom.

"The thoughts have got worse," he thought, "the evil little part of me seems much stronger. How the hell am I gonna cope on the outside? Last time I was free it wasn't long before the bastard thoughts made life a nightmare. I hope that I can get sorted before that happens again.

Maybe, I should get some professional help. I definitely ain't going back to Brookwood but there might be something else that can be done. Then again, I doubt it. I would rather be in prison than a mental hospital so it looks like a life inside.

What's the fucking point? Never get a bird; never have any luxuries. Fuck.... Fuck...... fuck.

I might as well give-up now. I haven't got anything to lose. This life ain't done me any favours."

Charlie was depressed, dejected, irrational. He turned the bed on its end, tore a strip from his sheet and fastened one end to the bed. He tied a noose. Nothing more to be done - he was ready.

"Come on, then" he urged himself, "things ain't gonna improve, are they?"

He hesitated. His nerve had deserted him. The moment had passed.

"Things could get better," he told himself, "where there's life, there's hope."

Charlie paced the cell.

"Nobody would understand," he thought. "How would anyone know what I was thinking?"

Charlie turned, now he could see the fence through the window.

"If I wasn't so ashamed of the bastard thoughts then I would find them easier to discuss."

He paced a few steps towards the barred window. The fence stood high, preventing most escape attempts.

"If only I could find someone to talk to, things would be much easier," he mused.

Charlie sat on his chair. Remorse was the strongest emotion.

"I feel gutted," he thought, "how could I let myself get in such a state?"

He wiped-away the final tear with a grubby shirt-sleeve.

"I'm not gonna let the bloody thoughts destroy me."

He replaced his bed and disposed of the torn sheeting.

"Whatever happens I have to fight these thoughts. I ain't gonna let them win."

Charlie calmed, little by little, as the minutes passed.

"I'm never gonna consider that option again. Things will improve. They have to."

Charlie was tired and confused. Maybe, when he woke, the situation would appear clearer. Now, all he wanted was to sleep.

He snuggled under his covers. The voices outside his window seemed to fade, more and more, as sleep came to his rescue.

Tomorrow he would be free from Feltham. Would he ever be free from himself?

Chapter 15

Charlie was a happy man when he walked free from Hollesley Bay. This occasion proved no different.

"Pucker," he mused, "this could be it. Free at last. Nothing to worry about except having a good time."

He strolled onwards looking for a familiar vehicle.

"No unpleasant thoughts, either."

He found a familiar vehicle.

"Hiya Lou" he shouted, "I'm glad you ain't late."

He climbed into the car and they headed for home.

"How's everyone?" asked Charlie.

"Much the same," answered Lucy, "but it did take Hazel a while to accept you were back in prison."

"That's okay, then" thought Charlie, "nobody's in the hump with me. I'd hate to go home and there was an atmosphere."

It wasn't long before the car stopped outside their home. Feltham was fairly local. Hazel's smile was warm and welcoming. She also looked puzzled and confused.

"How the hell can I expect her to understand my behaviour," thought Charlie, looking at his mother, "when I ain't got a clue myself."

The weekend passed. Charlie sat in his room, with a decent cup of coffee, watching television.

"This ain't exactly having a good time," he decided, "I might as well have stayed in prison."

He stretched and stood up.

"You have to give yourself time to adjust," he continued, "remember what happened on your last release? You certainly don't want a repeat performance."

Charlie walked to the window and peered out. The world was waiting.

"I must take things really slowly," he decided, "if I take it easy I might have a chance.

Of course, I'd love to go to a club and try my luck with some tart but I ain't ready. That really would be pushing my luck."

It was Sunday evening and Charlie was bored.

"When you are in prison," he mused, "you think of all the wonderful things you could be doing on the outside. Well, that ain't really the case. Most of the time you are bored out of your head."

The phone rang.

"That wouldn't happen in Feltham" Charlie smiled as he went to answer it.

"Hello, Charlie? It's Richard."

"Alright mate, how's it going?"

"Not bad.

Anyway, I'm in court tomorrow and I wondered if you fancied coming with me."

"Where?" asked Charlie.

"Dorking."

"What you done?"

"You know Darren Moss? Well, I gave him a bit of a slap."

Charlie glanced out the window. The world was waiting.

"I haven't been bothered by those bloody ideas," he thought, "and I really must try and do more than just sit in my room.

It would, also, be a nice thing to do - giving Richard a bit of moral support. I hope that he would do the same for me, if I asked."

"Okay mate, no problem" said Charlie, praying that he was making the right choice.

Richard and Charlie arrived at the court with plenty of time to spare.

"Richard has got a bad temper," thought Charlie, clambering out of the car, "and he likes a fight but, in the cold light of day, he will try and respect the law. He's the type of bloke who'd hit someone if they wound him up but I don't reckon you'd catch him doing a burglary."

They ventured into the courtroom. Richard went and bought some coffees. Charlie found some free seats.

"So far, so good" thought Charlie, glancing around the waiting room, "no old women."

Richard was called by his solicitor. He left Charlie drinking his coffee.

Charlie gazed at the defendants awaiting their fate.

"Most of them look like they are having a fun day out with their friends," he thought, "they don't look worried, in fact, you'd think they were on their way to a swingers' party."

One person, in particular, caught Charlie's eye.

"He doesn't look the type," thought Charlie, "he's like a fish out of water."

Charlie continued to stare.

"I could easily go and talk to him," he thought, "he ain't with anyone."

Charlie looked away.

"If I'm on my own I could easily have unwanted thoughts," he decided, "but if I'm talking to someone then I should be okay."

He strolled over to the young man and sat down.

"Hello" began Charlie, "you in court today or are you just waiting for someone?"

The tall, slim, clean-shaven, impeccably dressed youth didn't even sound like your average criminal.

"I'm appearing today," he spoke politely, his tone soft.

"Can't believe this bloke is in court," thought Charlie, "hope that I ain't talking to a nonce."

Charlie fidgeted in his seat.

"What you done then, mate?" he felt obliged to ask.

"I spent two months in America with someone else's credit card. I've been charged with fraud."

"Bloody hell," whistled Charlie, "what do they reckon you'll get?"

"I could go to prison, I suppose."

"Was the tone anxious or sad?" wondered Charlie. "This bloke wasn't your average thief. He seemed so gentle. I wonder why he did it. I don't reckon he'd have a nice time inside, with some of the shits you get in there."

Charlie and his new pal, Colin, chatted until Richard sauntered over to them.

The trio talked. Richard led the conversation. Charlie commented when necessary. Colin nodded and offered the occasional word.

"He's not at all confident in a group," decided Charlie, looking at Colin, "he might even be a little nervous."

It wasn't long before the loud speaker could be heard above the general babble.

"Miller. Court One."

"That's me," said Colin, with a nervous smile, "see you in a bit - hopefully."

Nobody had a chance to settle before another announcement could be heard.

"Hanson. Court Two."

Richard stood up and walked into the courtroom. Charlie watched from the public gallery. The case was short - one hundred and fifty pounds to be paid at twenty pounds a week.

"Not too bad" said Richard, standing in the waiting room.

"Yeah, could have been much worse," answered Charlie.

Colin walked out of Court One.

"Adjourned" he smiled.

"Fancy coming back with us for a coffee?" asked Charlie.

"Yeah thanks," replied Colin, "I'll follow you there."

"Great," thought Charlie, "Colin seems a really nice bloke and good pals are hard to find."

Colin and Charlie became firm friends. Colin could often be found at Charlie's house.

"I'm really glad I got to know Colin," thought Charlie, one afternoon after Colin had gone home, "I seem to be able to talk to him about anything."

Charlie flicked the switch on the kettle.

"I really trust Colin," he thought, "he never finds fault; he's just a loyal and supportive pal."

A week had passed since Colin's case had been adjourned. Charlie lay in bed trying to think of a reason to get-up.

"Might as well just lay here," he thought, "I've got nothing to do and if I do get-up the bastard thoughts will be right there."

There was a sharp tap at the back door.

"Now I have got a reason to get out of bed" decided Charlie, "I could ignore the door but, sooner or later, I'd die of boredom."

Charlie opened the door.

"Morning mate," grinned Colin, "didn't get you up, did I?"

"Don't worry," yawned Charlie, "can't stay in bed all day."

"Put the kettle on," suggested Colin.

"Okay mate," said Charlie.

"Hazel and Lucy both at work?" asked Colin

"Yeah," said Charlie, handing him a cup of coffee.

"You don't get out a lot, do you?" Colin made a chance remark.

"Should I tell him the truth," wondered Charlie, looking away from his pal, "what would he think? Would he still want to know me? I do trust him but is that enough?"

Charlie looked at his friend.

"Well, em....... you see......." Charlie stammered, "I find it very difficult to walk about in public places."

"What do you mean?" asked Colin, trying hard to understand.

"I get really nervous," answered Charlie, "I panic; sometimes I get so worked-up I'm physically ill."

"What makes you like that?" asked Colin, his tone curious.

"I can't be sure."

Colin looked at Charlie but said nothing.

"He knows I'm lying," thought Charlie, "I don't want him to think that I don't trust him."

Charlie rubbed his nose but didn't look at his friend.

"When I go out I have to grip my hands together," he said, "I just can't walk along normally."

"So," replied Colin, slowly, "if you took a walk down the road you would have to keep gripping your hands together?"

"Yeah, that's about it," answered Charlie

"So, what do you think your hands will do if they are not held together?" asked Colin.

"I...... em....... ain't sure," stammered Charlie, face flushed, ears burning.

Charlie rested his head on his arms. Colin took the hint and changed the subject.

"Got to go back to court in a month," he said, "might have to go to crown for sentence."

"Does your solicitor reckon you'll go in?"

"Could go either way," answered Colin.

Charlie made them both another cup of coffee.

"Look" began Colin, "if you find it so difficult to go outside why don't I come with you?"

Charlie considered the proposition.

"Can't do any harm," he mused, "and if I do have one of the bastard thoughts and start to worry about it then I can always check with Colin to see if anything has happened. He won't have to know exactly what I am worried about."

Charlie sipped his drink.

"Okay," he said, "thanks."

The idea of therapy walks had been born.

The following day Colin and Charlie stood in the kitchen ready for their first therapy session.

"All set," asked Colin, "now remember you must keep your hands by your sides."

"I'll do my best."

The two lads spent the next few hours marching up and down the road.

"Keep your hands apart," yelled Colin, each time Charlie gave-in to an unwanted idea.

The lads started to tire.

"Right," said Colin, "we'll start at the end of the street and walk to your house. You mustn't grip your hands together once."

"I'll try," answered Charlie.

The one mile hike began.

"Was an old woman there?" panicked Charlie, "did I hit her?"

Charlie walked-on, hands by his sides…. just.

"Calm down," he urged himself, "there's nobody about."

Charlie walked on with Colin about five paces behind.

"I've definitely got Colin in the best place," thought Charlie, "from where he is, he can see every move I make."

They neared the turning into Charlie's driveway.

"There's an old dear right beside you" the idea was strong, very strong.

The right hand was placed, quickly and firmly, in the grasp of the left.

"Oh shit," cursed Charlie.

"Looks like we've got to start again" said Colin, softly, "come-on."

Eventually therapy finished. Colin was pleased. Charlie was relieved.

Therapy sessions were a regular event.

Colin had just gone to see one of his old pals and Charlie sat in the kitchen with a hot coffee and a roll-up.

"Even though I'm doing all these walks," mused Charlie, "the intrusions seem to be getting worse and worse. I get lots more worries on the walks and I even have the bloody intrusions in the house.

Colin is brilliant, he does everything he can to make me feel better but it just ain't working. I don't know what more he could do but it just doesn't seem to be enough. Is there anything that anyone could do?"

Late one night, after a boring, depressing day, a dejected Charlie lay in bed. He stared at the ceiling, his hands folded behind his head. He lifted his head and stretched-out an arm to pick-up his glass of water.

"Oh hell," he cursed, "did I hit some old woman?"

Quick as lightening, as popular as rabies, the thought shook the disturbed youth.

"Get a grip" he told himself, "for fuck's sake, get a grip."

He put his hand back behind his head.

"How could some old woman be in your room without you even knowing about it?"

He rolled onto his front putting his hands beneath his chest.

"What if she crept in and I've just whacked her?"

Charlie was panicking. Logic just didn't apply. His heart raced, his mouth longed for the water, his chest ached, his stomach felt somebody was trying to rip it open.

"I hope that I ain't sick" panicked Charlie.

Gradually, very gradually, Charlie started to regain control.

Panic and fear was replaced by depression.

"Fuck this," moaned Charlie, "things can't get worse than this. Even when I'm in bed these bloody intrusions are destroying my life."

The room was dark, Charlie's mood was darker.

"I just can't carry-on like this," thought Charlie, "prison ain't perfect but it's got to be the best place to cope with these vile, fucking worries."

Charlie lay on the bed, his eyes brimming with tears.

"What about Colin?" he wondered. "Could he help? There was always the phone."

He rubbed a damp cheek with his hand.

"It's too late," he decided, "and, anyway, if I did speak to him I still ain't prepared to tell him exactly what I'm worried about. I'm scared that he'll hate me and tell everyone else about my problem."

A tear fell from Charlie's face.

"I'm all alone," he moaned, "I ain't got much fucking choice."

He stood up, threw on a jumper and a pair of grubby dungarees and went out to the garage. He picked-up his crowbar and torch. He left the house.

"I ain't sure what I'm going to do," he thought, shining his torch, "but I'll know what I'm looking for when I find it."

He had walked for a long time but he hadn't travelled far.

"Excuse me, sir," the voice boomed through the cold, night air, "could you stop there, please."

Charlie stopped.

"So what," he thought, "this is what I wanted, anyway."

Two constables hurried across the empty lane.

"Turn round and put your hands on the fence," they ordered.

They began the inevitable search.

"I don't care," decided Charlie, "what can they do to me? Give me a cure for the bloody thoughts?"

Charlie took his hands off the fence.

"Look, I'll save you the bother," he said, handing the crowbar to one of the policemen.

"You're under arrest. You do not have to say anything but……."

Charlie didn't listen to the rest of the caution. He'd heard it all before and, anyway, he had much more to worry about than being nicked for carrying a crowbar.

The officers led Charlie to their vehicle.

Charlie sat in a cell at the police station having been charged with going equipped to steal.

"I didn't have a choice," he decided, "I couldn't risk staying in society with the bloody intrusions in my mind. They seemed to be getting worse all the time. For all I know, I might have lost control, clouted some old dear and killed her."

He paced the cell.

"I wish people would understand," he thought, "this is the only way I can be sure that I ain't gonna do something really bad."

He sat on the bench.

"I'm sure that this is the only answer," he decided, "but how long will they keep asking the bloody question?"

Chapter 16

The following morning Charlie accepted the offer of a shower.

"No point going to court looking like a tramp" he decided.

He gasped as the icy water splashed against his body.

"I won't ask for bail," he reasoned, "so it won't be long before I'm back in Lewes. If I did apply for bail I would probably get it, but what then? More worries. Might as well stay in."

Lewes hadn't changed. First morning, first slop-out, first scrap.

"Fuck me," thought Charlie, watching the two prisoners, "ain't it amazing how easy it is to forget what it can be like."

A bulky lad, head shaven and face scarred, lashed at a smaller prisoner. The smaller lad had his head down to protect his face and, blindly, slashed with a razor. The larger inmate bled heavily. Instead of stopping the attack, these wounds seemed to increase the ferocity.

"Bloody hell" thought Charlie, "how long are the screws gonna let this carry on? 'Til one of 'em ends-up dead."

Other inmates watched; some nervous at seeing such savagery, some enjoying a good bit of entertainment.

"I'd avoid getting involved with something like that," decided Charlie, "but sometimes in places like this you ain't got no choice."

Finally, after what seemed like ages, the wardens poured onto the landing. The fight was stopped, the smaller prisoner had his blade taken, and the inmates were dragged from the wing.

"Screws didn't fuck about, did they?" said Charlie to Graham, "when they took his blade I thought they were gonna snap his arm."

Graham, a face from Charlie's previous visit, nodded. He was a tall, well-built, quietly-spoken young man.

"That little geezer," said Graham, "is always causing bother. He's a cocky little shit. Sooner or later he picks on the wrong person."

"Graham is such a calm customer," thought Charlie, "nothing seems to bother him. He's got a bit of a reputation in here - not to be messed with. I can see how he managed to get away with so many armed robberies before they nicked him."

"How long do you reckon you'll get?" asked Charlie, wanting to keep the conversation alive.

"I don't want to stand on my own" he thought, "that would make me an obvious target for anyone looking for grief. I ain't worried about having a scrap but I'll avoid it if I can. Anyway, I don't want to feel like Billy-no-mates."

"About nine years," answered Graham, "but my solicitor hopes he can get me a five. What about you?"

"Not much," said Charlie, "only done a bit of nicking."

"You wanker," thought Charlie, helpless to prevent one of the ever-powerful, ever-present intrusions.

Charlie's heart pounded. He couldn't concentrate. Nothing mattered other than his worry.

"I've got to get back to my cell, Graham," said Charlie, "I'll see you later."

Charlie sat on his bed.

"What the fuck am I going to do?" he panicked. "I just can't control my mind. It seems that I've a 'good me' and a 'bad me'. At the moment the 'good me' is stronger, but what if that changes?"

He crossed the cell to the barred window.

"I just don't know what will happen next," he thought, "and what's worse, I ain't got a clue what to do. Shall I just wait and see if I ever act on one of the unwanted ideas?"

Charlie stared out the tiny window.

"Wish I had a cell-mate," he thought, "I feel so bloody pissed-off. Maybe a bit of company would help."

"Why me," he mused, red mist rising, "I've tried everything to live with the ideas and they still try and destroy me."

Charlie heard a noise so he turned to look at the door. Four inmates stood at the entrance. One held a sock filled with something heavy as it hung by his side.

"A large battery or several little ones," decided Charlie.

Charlie stood still, waiting.

"Well, this is gonna be trouble," he thought, "but who gives a shit? What the hell have I got to lose? Things can't get any worse."

"Got anything for us," said the inmate holding the sock, an ugly little creep with an annoying face.

"Fuck yourself," snarled Charlie, "if you want anything, come and take it."

They walked towards him.

Charlie grabbed the nearest, punched him on the side of the face then bit his cheek. The teeth marks were visible on his face. Blood dripped. He yelped. His mates were loyal. They pulled Charlie onto the floor. They punched and kicked. They swore and shouted. Charlie rolled under his bed - he'd had enough. They left the cell, their point proved.

"Bastards," thought Charlie, checking his aching limbs, "still they couldn't make me feel any worse than I already do. And they've given me something to think about other than the bloody ideas."

Charlie stood up, slowly, and then flopped onto his bed.

"Okay," he mused, "I might be bruised and bleeding but I do feel calmer. I feel like I've been punished for having those awful thoughts."

Every seven days was a court appearance. Charlie never applied for bail.

"I don't think I should," he thought, after one court hearing, "I'm still getting unwanted thoughts in prison so I'd imagine they would be much worse if I was free."

It was a usual Saturday morning. Charlie was working-out in the gym with Terry.

"I feel quite good today," grunted Charlie, placing the barbell back on the stands.

"Yeah," agreed Terry, a tall, skinny lad with a mop of jet black hair. "When you've done your weights you feel that you've achieved something - you ain't just sat in the cell all fucking day."

Terry curled the barbell six times. The effort was etched on his face.

"You're on good form" encouraged Charlie. "You're biceps look ready to explode."

"What do you reckon Fisher, Mason and Brushfield are plotting?" asked Terry. "They've been whispering in the corner for the whole session."

"I dread to think," replied Charlie, glancing at the trio. "Somebody has probably upset them and they're planning their revenge. They're a nasty bunch of bastards and they really reckon they're the hardest posse on the landing."

"They look the part, in all," said Terry. "They're all tall, muscular, scarred and covered in tattoos."

"Don't worry, mate," said Charlie, "they wouldn't bother with us. We ain't done nothing to upset them."

Charlie and Terry worked on their biceps for the remainder of the session.

"That's it," shouted the orderly, "time's up. Go and get a shower."

Charlie gasped as the water splashed against his face. The washroom was packed, being such a small area. Charlie looked across at Terry, a couple of feet away. He was chatting to Simon Walsh, a seventeen-year-old car thief.

"From what I know of Walshie," thought Charlie, washing his shoulders, "he's a nice lad. A bit mouthy, but, apart from that, a genuinely decent bloke."

Charlie hardly noticed Fisher, Mason and Brushfield until they grabbed a shocked, frightened Walsh.

"You owe us an ounce of burn, Walsh," snarled Fisher, as Mason and Brushfield held the lad against the wall.

Walsh had his face pressed against the stone wall and his arms were stretched-out either side. He was helpless. The other prisoners moved away. They didn't want Fisher to think they were siding with the enemy.

"What the fucking hell are they gonna do to him?" panicked Charlie, stomach churned-up and spat-out. "They're not gonna rape him, are they? Sick bastards. And all this because of an ounce of burn."

Charlie inched forward, scared almost to death.

"God no" he quivered, "what do I do? I feel like I'm back in the bogs with the fuckers who attacked me."

He inched further forward, wanting to run in the opposite direction.

"What if I yelled," he thought, tasting vomit, "surely the screws would come in. Okay, I'd be known as a grass but that's better than

169

watching a young lad being shagged. Why the fuck ain't nobody else doing anything?"

He must have got closer; he could see something in Fisher's hand - a razor blade melted onto the end of a toothbrush.

"Oh, thank fuck" thought Charlie, faint with relief, "they ain't gonna shag his arse, just cut it."

Fisher slashed madly at Walsh's naked flesh. Walsh, faced still pressed against the wall, moaned quietly. The water turned red as it dripped to the shower floor. Walsh's arse was lines of dark red, with paler red in between.

The punishment ended. Fisher and his two henchmen left the showers, smirking.

"Fisher must have hidden the blade in his pubes," decided Charlie, "I couldn't see it when they walked away."

Walsh staggered out of the showers, blood flowed from his wounds. A trail of diluted blood marked his path. It took little time for the water to hide the savagery.

Two wardens rushed into the showers.

"What happen to Walsh?" asked Mr. Holmes, "who the fuck did that to him?"

"Didn't see anything" chorused those inmates still in the shower.

"Right then" shouted Mr. Holmes "fucking get dressed."

"Vicious bastards," thought Charlie, throwing on his clothes, "I wish I'd had the bottle to get involved. If Walsh was a close mate I'd have had to jump-in, however much I was crapping myself. Trouble is, you go against someone like Fisher and you're on protection with all the nonces. Look at Walsh, forgot to pay back some burn and the poor shit's in hospital."

Charlie was still trembling as he walked back to the wing with Terry.

Canteen was the highlight of the week. Tuesday morning and Charlie wandered down the steps to the second landing looking forward to buying some tobacco.

"Hello Charlie," said Alex, an adult prisoner on the third landing.

"Hello mate," answered Charlie, remembering the old convict from a previous sentence.

"How's it going?" asked Alex, "when did you get back?"

"Oh, I ain't been back long," said Charlie, "soon got back into the old routine."

"You want to get yourself sorted," said Alex, "this ain't a good way of life for anyone."

Charlie rubbed his nose, not quite sure how to answer.

"If you keep getting put-away," continued Alex, "you'll soon have nothing left other than in here."

"I do know what you mean," replied Charlie.

"Look at me," said Alex. "I'm sixty-one and I've spent the last twenty years emptying a piss-pot. That's a fucking waste."

"Yeah," mumbled Charlie.

"I was an alcoholic, that's why I started coming to prison" said Alex, "and I never got myself sorted."

"I see," mumbled Charlie, looking at the floor.

"You must know why you are here," lectured Alex, "if you don't help yourself you'll end-up like me."

"Yeah."

"I'm only trying to warn you," said Alex, "don't waste your life in places like this."

"Yeah."

"Anyway, you'd better hurry," said Alex, "or the fucking shop will be closed."

"Thanks mate," mumbled Charlie, politely. "I won't forget what you have told me."

Alex's sadness covered his wrinkled face and reflected from his dark green eyes.

Charlie only just got to the canteen before it closed.

That night, after lock-up, Charlie lay on his unmade bed gazing at the bars on the tiny window.

"Old Alex has definitely got a point," he reasoned, "there is often a reason why a person turns to crime. My problem is the unwanted thoughts. I want to feel safe, secure, normal and that is easier in prison."

Charlie stood up and walked to his table in the corner of the cell.

"I have to get it sorted," he decided, "that's what Alex said."

Charlie poured a glass of water from his jug.

"Easier said than done."

Charlie took a gulp of the water.

"How?" he wondered aloud.

Charlie finished the drink and sat on his bed.

"Okay," he said to himself, "let's look at the facts."

He lay down.

"The thoughts are horrible," he thought, "but I have never acted on any of them. I have never hit an old woman and never spoken aloud when an unwanted idea has entered my head. So, doesn't it follow the thoughts only exist in my head? Surely, I'm not going to start attacking old women when I get out."

Charlie scratched his head.

"The thoughts really do bother me," he mused, hope rising, "but I'm positive that I ain't a threat to anyone. I'm surely not a danger to society. The only person I would upset is myself."

Charlie sat on the end of his bed.

"Surely," he wondered, "if I was to explain everything to Dr. King then he might be able to help me. He might be able to give me some pills. I'm not going back to Brookwood but there might be some other help available."

Charlie felt more positive than he had in a long while.

"At least I've got a plan" he thought, "something to aim for."

He lay back down. Happy thoughts floated through his mind as he drifted into a restful sleep. He hadn't even removed his dungarees.

Dorking Magistrates' Court entertained many offenders. This windy, rainy day it was Charlie's turn. Charlie sat in the large cell waiting for his solicitor.

"This is it," he pondered, "I've got to get out of prison and get my life sorted. I can't keep running away."

Eventually Mr. Gordon arrived.

"Sorry I'm late, Mr. Lloyd" he apologised, not looking at all sorry, "bit of car trouble, I'm afraid."

"I want to apply for bail" said Charlie, coming straight to the point, "I've done a lot of thinking and I've decided that I've already wasted too much of my life."

"As you wish," replied Mr. Gordon, "and as the Charge isn't that serious, I feel that we are in with a fighting chance."

Charlie paced the length of the cell, fifteen steps.

"I hope Dr. King can get me sorted" he thought, "and won't it be great to see Colin again."

"Hang-on, you ain't got bail yet," he reminded himself.

"I feel lucky," he spoke aloud.

Finally, the door was unlocked.

"You ready, Charlie?" said John the jailer.

"As I'll ever be, guv."

Mr. Gordon made a thorough and efficient application.

"He's good," thought Charlie, sitting in the dock, "very professional. Could put a bit more emotion into it but I ain't got no complaints. He just tells them how it is - you don't spent ages in prison for walking about with a crowbar. He ain't gonna have them in tears but he seems to know the law."

The prosecution objected to bail.

"This young man is very likely to commit further offences if he is released" droned the short, fat, balding prosecution solicitor, "he was arrested only days after release from a previous term in custody......"

Charlie's mind wandered.

"What a miserable bastard" he thought, "just because he ain't got nothing going for him, he wants every other fucker to be depressed."

The prosecution's case concluded.

It didn't take the magistrates' long to decide. They granted bail.

Charlie's mother was sitting in the waiting room.

"She doesn't know why I'm always in trouble," thought Charlie, when he spotted her, "it's amazing she's still talking to me. I know how much she hates thieves."

Charlie climbed out of his mother's car at the top of the driveway.

"I've got to make it work" he thought, "I can't let the unwanted ideas destroy me. I've got to get help and live a normal life."

He looked at his mother as she got out the other side of the car.

"I mustn't go back to prison, I bloody mustn't."

Once inside, Charlie headed straight for the bathroom.

"Washing prison away," he thought, enjoying a hot soak, "hopefully this'll be the last time."

Charlie was ready to face the world. First job - phone Colin.

"Hello mate, guess who? Got a bit of bail."

"Great," said Colin, genuinely thrilled, "I'll get round right now."

The purring of a finely tuned engine and Colin had arrived.

"I'll put the kettle on," said Charlie.

"Lovely," replied Colin.

The two young men sat, drank and talked.

"So you're pleased to be free?" asked Colin.

"No problems, so far."

"And how's your...... em....... difficulties been?"

"Well" answered Charlie, "before I went in they were terrible. I suppose I just gave up fighting and did anything I could to get away from them. Prison seemed the only answer."

"You should have told me it had got so bad," said Colin.

"I know," replied Charlie, "but it all happened so fast I didn't have time to think. I was bloody desperate."

"And what about now?" questioned Colin.

"I seem to have things under control," replied Charlie, "but I ain't sure how long that will last."

"So you can leave the house and go out?" asked Colin.

"I think so," said Charlie, after a moment's hesitation.

"Well then" said Colin, "if you feel okay we could go out tonight and have a little celebration."

Charlie couldn't fail to notice Colin's eager expression.

"Oh no" he thought, "I don't want to let him down, he's such a decent pal but can I cope? The bloody intrusions could ruin the whole night."

Colin sensed his friend's anxiety.

"If we go out," he said, "and you feel nervous we'll just come home. We haven't got to stay 'til closing time."

"I can't let the bloody intrusions control every decision I make," decided Charlie, "or I might have well stayed in the cooler. And Colin ain't the type of bloke to start arguing if I tell him I want to go home."

"Okay then, Colbo," he said. "Why not?"

174

Chapter 17

Charlie sat in the kitchen, dressed in his best clothes.

"Colin will be here soon," he mused, "I'll feel better when I ain't on my own."

Charlie paced the kitchen floor.

"Things will be fine," he encouraged himself, "just concentrate on having a good time."

Colin pulled-up on time.

"Jump in" he said, opening the passenger's door, "I know the ideal place."

A ten minute drive and they sat in a quiet pub.

"This ain't too bad, is it?" asked Colin.

"No, it's fine," replied Charlie, "do you want another drink?"

"Well, we could go to a club," suggested Colin, "should be plenty of talent. Would you be okay?"

Charlie hesitated.

"Most blokes, just out of prison, would love the chance to go to a club with loads of crumpet," he pondered, "but when you have to worry about unwanted ideas it's a slightly different story."

Colin sensed that Charlie was having doubts.

"Remember," he said, "if you feel edgy then we'll leave."

"Okay then," replied Charlie.

The atmosphere felt electric. Colin and Charlie gazed round the room to see which of the talent was available.

"Wouldn't it be good if we could pull" thought Charlie, "I ain't had a bird for ages."

Charlie noticed a couple snogging in the corner. The lad's hands wandered towards the girl's bottom.

"Lucky sod" thought Charlie, "I know she's a dog but I wouldn't say no."

Colin tapped Charlie on the shoulder.

"Will you be okay if I leave you on your own?" he asked.

"Yeah okay."

Colin wandered into the crowd. He spoke briefly to a couple of young lovelies. Abruptly, he returned.

"They're not interested," he said.

Charlie glanced round the club.

"What about those two" he said, pointing at the targets.

"Bit rough," replied Colin, eyes wandering round the room.

"They're not that bad," urged Charlie.

"I wouldn't fancy seeing that naked first thing in the morning" said Colin, "I've seen smaller hippos."

"Look" argued Charlie, "you can have the best one."

"That is the best one." answered Colin.

"Go on" persuaded Charlie, "if we leave it too long they'll be snapped-up."

"You have been away a long time, haven't you?" grinned Colin, "okay then, but nobody can ever accuse me of not doing enough for Charity."

Colin swerved through the crowds towards the two young ladies.

"Okay," thought Charlie, watching his mate, "they are fat but I really couldn't care."

Colin didn't seem to have any problem starting a conversation. One girl chatted, the other looked bored.

Charlie, feeling like a spare part, walked towards the gathering.

"What the bloody hell should I do?" he wondered, "go and start talking or just stand here and watch?"

He needn't have worried. The girl, ignored by Colin, came over.

"I'm Emma" she said, "my friend seems a little pre-occupied, so is it okay if I talk to you?"

"Yeah…. em…….sure," stuttered Charlie, far from comfortable, "I'm …. em….. Charlie,"

"Would you like a drink?" offered Emma.

"Eh….. yeah……. ta" stammered Charlie, not finding things any easier.

"I'll have a glass of wine," she said, handing Charlie twenty pounds, "get yourself whatever you want."

"Blimey," thought Charlie, "intelligent, confident and generous. She ain't gonna want to know me."

"Right….. yeah…… sure," mumbled Charlie, feeling out of his depth.

It didn't take long to get served. He walked over to Emma and handed her a glass of red wine.

"I'll just get your change," he said, hand diving into his pocket.

"Don't worry about that," said Emma, "keep it."

"Pardon" said Charlie, certain his ears were playing tricks.

"Keep it," repeated Emma.

"You sure," said Charlie, unaware he'd gone to Heaven.

"Course I am" she said, with a lovely smile.

"She might be a bit fat," thought Charlie, smiling at Emma, "but she's got a lovely face. Ain't it amazing how a bit of extra weight doesn't matter when you get to know someone."

Emma paid for everyone's drinks - she really was a very generous young lady.

It was nearing the end of a lovely evening.

"I've just come out of prison," said Charlie to Emma, believing honesty to be the best policy.

"What did you do?" she asked, seemingly unfazed.

"Bit of thieving, nothing too serious," answered Charlie.

"That's nothing to worry about," said Emma, "so long as you're not a sex offender."

"Needn't have waited 'til the end of the night," thought Charlie, "she ain't gonna make an excuse and get lost. In fact, she doesn't seem bothered at all."

"Why did you do it?" asked Emma.

"Not sure really," replied Charlie, believing honesty not to be the best policy, "no money, I guess."

"Oh right," answered Emma, flashing that lovely smile, "I see."

"I definitely ain't gonna tell her about the intrusive thoughts," decided Charlie, "that would be one way to blow my chances."

Last orders were called.

"Is it okay if we come back with you?" asked Colin.

"He's changed his tune," thought Charlie, "he's certainly doing his bit for charity."

"Unfortunately we're staying the night at a friend's," answered Emma.

"Shit," thought Charlie, "I definitely wouldn't have said no. I hope prison didn't ruin my chances."

Charlie stared at Emma.

"Nothing ventured, nothing gained," he decided.

"Can I take your phone number," he said, still looking at Emma.

"Actually," answered Emma, "we're not on the phone at the moment......."

"Oh no," thought Charlie, "and I reckoned she was keen."

"But," she continued, "I'll give you my work number. Please call me there on Monday."

"Pucker," thought Charlie, "cracked-it."

The days flew passed. Charlie and Colin enjoyed much of their spare time with Emma and her pulling partner, Lisa.

"It's really good that Emma and Lisa are both loaded," said Charlie to Colin as they drove to the girls' flat.

"I know mate," replied Colin, "they don't mind paying for everything when we go out."

It was a rainy evening, a month or so after Charlie's release. The foursome was having a quiet drink in the girls' local.

Charlie, bored with Colin's jokes, glanced round the bar. His eyes rested on an elderly woman sipping a gin and tonic.

"Oh hell" he panicked, "did I hit her?"

The idea had been born. Now it would grow into a fully formed adult before it could be buried.

"You okay, Charlie," asked Emma, concerned by his change in behaviour, "you look like you've seen a ghost."

"Sorry," replied Charlie, "just don't feel brilliant."

Charlie stared at the old woman. She was still drinking her gin and tonic.

"She doesn't look like she has been clouted," thought Charlie, "in fact she looks just fine."

When Charlie took his eyes off the woman his anxiety levels would increase. His heart raced, his hands shook slightly, his mouth dried and his eyes blurred. When he checked the lady in question, he would calm considerably. Several minutes passed and Charlie started to relax. Now, he didn't have to keep his constant vigil. All the same, the occasional glance didn't do any harm. Sooner or later the worry could be buried. The memory could not. Charlie felt depressed.

"Could this be the beginning of the end?" he panicked, "what if the bloody intrusions start to control my whole life again?"

178

Charlie glanced at Colin. His friend's concern was obvious.

"Do you mind if we leave?" asked Charlie. "I feel terrible."

"No problem" answered Colin, "I'm ready now."

The worries were frequent over the following days and weeks. Some were bad, others worse. Charlie stayed at home, finding it easier that way. Emma popped-in occasionally. Colin was there most of the time.

"I'm quite concerned," thought Hazel, glancing at her son, "things are definitely going from bad to worse. If something isn't sorted-out soon I fear the worst. He'll end-up back in prison. I must get him some professional help."

Hazel managed to contact Dr. King.

"Yes," said Dr. King, "I'll see Charlie as an out-patient and I'll do everything possible to avoid a return to Brookwood Hospital."

Charlie agreed to see the doctor.

"What other options have I got," he pondered, "there just might be something he can do."

Within days Charlie sat opposite the psychiatrist.

"I really hope that he can help," thought Charlie, "what the bloody hell will I do if he says that there's nothing he can do?"

"So you didn't like Brookwood?" began Dr. King.

"No, I'm not going back there," said Charlie, showing his agitation.

"Okay," soothed the doctor, "now, tell me about your problem."

"Well...... em......." Charlie struggled to explain. "It seems that part of me keeps putting unwanted suggestions in my head."

Charlie glanced at the doctor. His expression gave little away.

"And?" said Dr. King.

"Em...... well...... I suppose," said Charlie, "it would be more accurate to say that the unwanted thoughts make me check that I haven't done something."

"Explain" said the doctor.

"Well I have to keep checking things to make sure I haven't acted on an unwanted idea."

"When you use the word 'unwanted'," said the doctor, "please could you clarify."

"Well," replied Charlie, "consciously, I don't invite these ideas; they are just there, in my mind."

"You have no control over them?" asked Dr. King.

"I don't seem to," answered Charlie.

"Do the ideas take the form of another person's voice?" asked the psychiatrist.

"No," replied Charlie, "the only voice I hear is my own."

"Okay," said Dr. King, calmly, "what do these ideas make you think that you have done?"

Charlie hesitated.

"He's gonna think that I'm a right shit," he thought.

"It's okay," said the doctor, smiling, "I'm certain that I won't be shocked by anything you can tell me."

"Well….. em….. I always worry that I've hit an old woman," Charlie blurted.

"Have you ever hit an old woman?" asked the doctor.

"No," answered Charlie, "and I never would."

"But you often think that you have?" asked Dr. King.

"The ideas make me check that I haven't," answered Charlie, thoughtfully.

"Do you have to check more than once?"

"Many times," said Charlie.

"Do these ideas and the checking dominate your day to day living?" asked the doctor.

"Some days I can't concentrate on anything but the ideas," replied Charlie.

"Does that affect your mental state?"

"Well, I feel really anxious most of the time. Depressed, sometimes angry, when I have an unwanted idea but, then, really happy when I've checked the idea."

"I see," said Dr. King.

"I was worried that I was schizophrenic," blurted Charlie.

"You're not schizophrenic," stated Dr. King, inspiring hope and confidence.

"I won't have to go back to hospital?" asked Charlie.

"No," replied Dr. King, "I'll try you on some pills. They should ease the intrusive thoughts. Come back and see me next week."

"So, do you know what's wrong with me?" asked Charlie, scared of the answer but desperate to find out.

Dr. King cleared his throat.

"Em…." he said, "I would call your condition obsessive neurosis."

Charlie looked puzzled.

"What's that," he thought, "sounds quite serious."

"You might have heard of 'OCD' or obsessive compulsive disorder," said Dr. King, attempting to clarify his diagnosis.

"Will I ever be normal?" asked Charlie, feeling it best to be prepared for the worst.

"We'll work on it," said the doctor, "and you should feel better with the medication."

Charlie would have talked all day. He wasn't given the chance.

"See you next week" said Dr. King.

Charlie left the room. He glanced at the prescription - 'sulpiride'.

"Never heard of them," he thought, "I just hope they can help. Whatever happens, things can't get much worse."

Charlie felt intoxicated. His vision was blurred and walking in a straight line was more than he could manage. Sulpiride seemed to be a very powerful drug.

"This feels bloody strange," thought Charlie, staggering towards the kettle, "I feel like I've downed ten pints. Nothing seems to matter. I feel relaxed, so relaxed my body won't work properly - but who cares? I certainly don't."

Charlie had been taking the drugs, religiously, for a couple of days. He sat in the kitchen, with a roll-up and a cup of coffee, very relaxed.

"I still get the unwanted ideas," thought Charlie, "they haven't stopped but they don't seem to bother me. I don't seem to worry about the ideas that much. Usually, after a few minutes, I've forgotten what worried me in the first place."

Colin continued to be a great help. The therapy walks improved dramatically.

"This ain't so bad," thought Charlie, strolling along the road with Colin, "I'm not very stressed at all. Yeah, the worries flicker through my mind but they don't cause me that much bother."

Charlie and Colin ended a therapy walk.

"That was okay," thought Charlie, "no real problems. Ain't modern medicine bloody amazing."

Charlie's days drifted past.

"These pills certainly help" thought Charlie, popping two of the little white tablets, "I feel constantly pissed. Nothing seems to bother me. I must be the most laid-back person in the world."

Charlie lounged at the kitchen table.

"What shall I do?" he thought, "Colin ain't about and I feel bloody bored."

The phone rang. Charlie leapt into life.

"Saved by the bell," he thought, "ain't it amazing how the smallest thing can brighten your day when you are bored?"

He grabbed the phone.

"Hello."

"Hello Chaz, it's me Ed."

"Hello mate, how's it going?"

"Not too bad. Do you remember the night you and Colin went down the pub?" asked Edward.

"Yeah," answered Charlie.

"Well" said Ed, "this bird I know, Linda, saw you in the pub and she's quite keen. Anyway, she wants to know if you fancy popping round to Proctor Gardens to see her one evening."

"You're winding me up," said Charlie.

"I promise you," answered Edward.

Charlie hesitated.

"Look" said Ed, "don't worry about Emma, she ain't gonna know."

"What's this Linda like?" asked Charlie.

"She ain't too bad," replied Ed, "quite a nice girl."

"I suppose that I could," thought Charlie, "the pills are helping me and my therapy walks with Colin are going really well. I could look at this Linda as therapy - see if I'm well enough to visit her on my own. There ain't no need to tell Emma anything because Linda will only be a friend - I ain't gonna jump on her."

"Okay then," said Charlie, "I ain't got nothing to lose. What number's her flat?"

"Forty-eight," said Ed, "I'll tell her you'll be round soon."

The following Tuesday was cold and wet. At five o'clock Charlie phoned Emma, telling her he was going out with Colin. At seven o'clock he was tapping on the door of flat forty-eight.

"I feel really bad about Emma," he thought, standing on the doorstep, "she's a lovely girl. If I had no intention of doing anything with this Linda then why did I lie to Emma?"

The door opened.

"Hi," grinned Charlie, studying the girl. "Nothing special," he thought, "plain, slightly overweight, and hair looks a bit greasy."

"Hello" she drawled.

"Should I be doing this," thought Charlie, "it's not too late to make an excuse and leave."

"Come in" she offered.

"Oh, what the hell" decided Charlie, "I ain't gonna do nothing and it's only one night."

Charlie walked into the small flat, following Linda to the living room. He sat down and opened one of the cans of beer he had brought.

"Don't really know what to say," thought Charlie. "I'll just sit here and have a few drinks."

He downed three of the cans.

"I'm here now, might as well make the most of it."

"Is it right you've just left prison?" said Linda.

"Yeah," answered Charlie.

He scratched his head, trying to think of something intelligent.

"How many children have you got?" he asked.

"Two. Becky and Alan."

"What happened to their dad?" he asked.

"Well, we were married" she replied, "but he had an affair when I was pregnant with Alan so we split."

They talked and drank.

"She's okay, I suppose," mused Charlie, "it ain't her fault her husband had an affair. She's had lots of blokes since then but that's probably because people have just used her for a shag. It's got to be a lot harder to meet somebody when you've already got a couple of kids."

The more Charlie drank, the better things seemed.

"It's good that Linda lives locally," he thought, "I wouldn't mind coming round to see her again."

Charlie knew that he'd had enough to drink.

"I really shouldn't have another can," he thought.

Before too long, he'd drunk all the alcohol he'd brought to Linda's flat.

"She's a real stunner," he decided, looking at Linda through glazed eyes.

Charlie didn't leave Linda's flat until the morning.

Charlie, as he had promised in a drunken stupor, visited regularly. He met Becky and Alan but, inexperienced with young children, found them hard to handle.

Charlie dragged himself out of bed. He'd stayed at Linda's flat until quite late the night before so he wasn't surprised it was almost midday.

"I think that I'll only visit Linda when her kids are in bed" thought Charlie, "because I just can't be bothered with them."

Charlie still kept in contact with Emma. One night, having spent a pleasant evening with the young lady, he sat at the kitchen table.

"I do like Emma," he thought, "but we just ain't got anything in common. She's a successful girl with great prospects, whereas I'm just a loser. Maybe I should stick with Linda - we seem to have much more in common."

Charlie made himself a cup of coffee. "Colin hardly ever sees Lisa," he thought. "Reckons you should shag as many different women as you can. I wonder if he'll ever settle?"

Charlie rolled a cigarette. Smoking helped him make important decisions.

"I doubt," he pondered, "if I'll see much more of Emma. It was good, bloody good, while it lasted but it just ain't going anywhere."

He blew a ring of smoke and watched as it disappeared.

"I reckon she feels the same," decided Charlie. "Trouble is, she's too polite to say anything."

Charlie felt tired. He needed his bed.

The 'OCD' simmered beneath the surface.

"I know that I've still got my problem," he thought, one boring Thursday afternoon, "but I reckon my medication will keep it under control. The unwanted ideas are still there but, with the tablets, I can deal with them."

Charlie and his mother visited the psychiatrist every week. Hazel waited in the games room while Charlie saw Dr. King.

"So, how are things?" asked Dr. King.

"Not too bad," replied Charlie, "I still get worries but they don't bother me as much as they used to. I was in the newsagents' the other day when I saw an old lady. I did worry that I'd clouted her but the thought didn't control me for as long as I was expecting. In fact, it was a matter of minutes before I had got myself under control."

"That's what we are hoping for," said Dr. King, "but you must continue to expose yourself to the situations that because you anxiety. Eventually these situations should become less threatening. The sulpiride should help you to keep calm and in control."

"Oh yeah," Charlie said, "I've got to go to court for sentencing."

"When is that?" asked Dr. King.

"Next week."

"And what was the charge?"

"Going equipped to steal."

"I'll write you a report. Who is your solicitor?"

"Mr. Gordon," answered Charlie.

"Fine," said Dr. King. "See you next time."

The day arrived.

"Ain't it strange," thought Charlie, throwing on some clothes, "nice things like Christmas seem to take ages to get here but crap things get here faster than Ed can pull a bird."

Charlie, his mother and Linda arrived at Dorking Magistrates'.

"I don't feel that nervous," thought Charlie. "That's probably got lots to do with the amount of sulpiride I've taken."

Charlie spotted Colin almost as soon as he swaggered into the court's waiting room.

"Brilliant," he thought, cheering considerably, "a bit more genuine support. The more the merrier."

"Bit nervous mate?" asked Colin.

"Yeah," admitted Charlie. "I'm going to ask for a conditional discharge. I ain't doing probation or anything. If they won't give me a conditional discharge then they'll have to send me to prison."

"You should be okay," muttered Colin.

"Even my best pal reckons I'll get put away," thought Charlie, "things ain't looking too rosy."

"Mr. Lloyd, could you come with me," said Mr. Gordon, approaching the group.

Charlie nodded and followed the smartly-dressed solicitor to an empty room.

"So what are we going to ask for today?" said Mr. Gordon.

"A conditional discharge," answered Charlie.

"We would be most fortunate to receive so light a sentence considering your past convictions," said Mr. Gordon."

"Have you got Dr. King's report?" asked Charlie.

"I have," replied Mr. Gordon, "and it'll certainly count in your favour but why not consider probation as an option?"

"No," replied Charlie, adamantly, "I want a conditional discharge. Anything else and I'll just keep being reminded of all this shit. I'd rather go inside, do my time and then sort out my life. With Dr. King's help I'll make it."

"Well, I can't promise," conceded Mr. Gordon, "but, we'll do our best. See you in court."

Charlie returned to his small, loyal gathering. "Just have to wait and see what happens," he sighed.

"Lloyd; court one," the voice crackled across the waiting room.

Charlie followed the usher into the court and took his position in the dock. His mother, Colin and Linda sat in the public gallery. The prosecuting solicitor stood up, outlined the charge, and then sat down. Enter Mr. Gordon.

"I really feel," said Mr. Gordon, "that my client should be given the chance to re-shape his life under the guidance of Dr. King."

Dr. King's report was submitted.

Mr. Gordon concluded his strong defence.

The magistrates retired, each clutching a copy of the psychiatric report.

Charlie, seated in the dock, waited. "I wonder what they'll think when they read Dr. King's report," he thought. "I ain't sure why I feel so nervous. Probably because I really want to make something of my life. I reckon that with Dr. King's help I'll be able to get sorted. With Colin and Dr. King in my corner I have a chance."

The magistrates returned. Nothing was given away by the blank expressions on their faces.

"We'd like to hear Mr. Lloyd."

Charlie stood in the dock.

"Mr. Lloyd," began the presiding magistrate, "given your condition wouldn't Brookwood Hospital be the best place for you?"

"Definitely not, sir," replied Charlie. "I believe I'd get worse in hospital. Most of the patients function way below normal. Some are so drugged they don't function at all. I really think that Dr. King can treat me without me going to hospital. If I'm worried I'm going to commit a crime then I'll go and see him."

The magistrates had listened intently.

"We shall retire."

"I wonder how long they'll be," thought Charlie, sitting in the dock, eyes focused forwards. "I reckon they believed what I said, probably because I was telling the truth."

The magistrates returned. Once again, expressions were blank.

"Mr. Lloyd," began the presiding magistrate, clearing his throat, "after careful consideration we have decided to grant a conditional discharge with the agreement that you continue to visit Dr. King as an out-patient."

Charlie, very relieved, ambled from the dock.

"This is it," decided Charlie, grinning at Colin, "a chance to beat these bloody thoughts."

Charlie, his mother, Linda and Colin left the courtroom.

"How do you feel?" asked Colin.

"Like a weight has been lifted from my shoulders, now I can concentrate on the problems in hand" answered Charlie.

The group headed from the court in the direction of the car park.

"Now I really have got a chance," thought Charlie. "Colin, a loyal pal, to help me with therapy. Hazel, who will do anything to keep me out of prison even if it's only to avoid the shame of it.

Linda, possibly not the love of my life but at least it shows I can have a relationship."

"The car park is just round the corner," said Hazel.

"Jolly good, answered Charlie. They walked, happily, onwards. "And," mused Charlie, "I've got a bloody good doctor who seems to have got me on the best pills. Yeah, I really reckon I can do it. No more prison. I won't need it. No more people getting slashed, no more beatings, no more piss-pot washes and no more shit grub. Now, it'll be beating my fears: a good job, plenty of money, good mates and a nice bird."

"You okay, Chaz?" said Colin.

"Never better, mate," answered Charlie.

They turned the corner. Charlie's arm nudged someone. He turned his head. An old woman plodded along the path.

"Oh hell," panicked Charlie, heart hammering against his chest, "what the hell have I done?"

Printed in the United Kingdom
by Lightning Source UK Ltd.
101468UKS00001B/34